Beyond Spirituality

TEACHINGS OF AN INDIAN SAINT ON ECONOMIC EMPOWERMENT

SARNGADHARAN M

SARAT SARNGADHARAN

Clever Fox® PUBLISHING

Chennai • Bangalore

CLEVER FOX PUBLISHING
Chennai, India

Published by CLEVER FOX PUBLISHING 2025

ISBN: 978-93-6707-976-8

About the Authors

Dr. M. Sarngadharan is a distinguished economist specializing in financial management. His influential works, including "Financial Analysis for Management Decisions" and "Indian Economy in the Globalized World," have significantly advanced the field.

Dr. Sarngadharan holds a first-class first rank in M.Com. from the University of Kerala and a Ph.D. from the University of Calicut. He has successfully mentored over 30 doctoral students during his distinguished academic career, serving as Professor, Head of Department, and Dean at the University of Kerala.

Beyond academia, Dr. Sarngadharan has served on numerous expert committees, contributing to policy formulation. He is a recipient of the prestigious Dr. Ambedkar Legal Studies Award. He was ICSSR Senior Fellow at the esteemed Gulati Institute of Finance and Taxation. His research has been presented at numerous international conferences.

Sarat Sarngadharan is a highly accomplished Technology Leader with two decades of experience in delivering innovative software solutions and managing finances. He excels at leading and mentoring high-performing teams, driving impactful results, and championing innovation.

Sarat Sarngadharan has a proven track record of successfully leading globally distributed teams across multiple multinational companies. Currently based in the US, he serves as a Technology Leader for a major healthcare player.

He holds an MBA in Finance from Central European University, Budapest, Hungary, and a BTech in Electronics & Communication from the University College of Engineering, Kerala, India.

Furthermore, he authored the opening chapter, "Change Management Strategies for Enhanced Working Results," in the book "Entrepreneurship in the Globalized World." He led the CEU Business School team to victory in the Divisional Championship of the International Business Competition in San Diego, US, showcasing his leadership and strategic acumen.

Contents

About the Authors *iii*
Foreword *vii*

1. A Blueprint for the Future: Economic Vision of the Guru 1
2. Building Stronger Organizations: The Guru's Vision of Unity and Collective Action 6
3. Conquering Poverty: The Guru's Path to Prosperity 16
4. Education as Wealth, Service as Purpose: The Guru's Vision 29
5. Igniting Industry: A Call to Action 34
6. Unlocking Growth: The Power of Micro, Small, and Medium Enterprises for Economic Growth 40
7. The Art of Management: Leadership Lessons from the Guru 46
8. Creating Opportunities: Employment and Income for All 52
9. Nourishing the Nation: Strengthening Agriculture 63
10. The Sivagiri Model: A Vision for Agro-Industrial Development 70
11. Business at the Core: Exploring Economic Themes at Sivagiri 77
12. The Digital Age: From Barter to Bytes 85

13. Collective Strength: Joint Stock Companies for Growth 89

14. The Cooperative Way: Empowering Communities through Collaboration 99

15. Funding the Future: Banks and Entrepreneurial Support 106

16. The Guru's Legacy: Financial Institutions for the People 112

17. Harmony in Action: Cooperation between Employees and Management 123

18. A Model for Labor: Organizing for Equity and Dignity 134

19. Sustainability and Prosperity: Cleanliness and Nature Conservation 142

20. Prudence and Progress: Avoiding Complacency on the Path to Success 148

21. Inspired by the Sage: Success Stories of the Guru's Disciples 158

22. Epilogue: The Sivagiri Pilgrimage – A Perpetual Cycle of Learning 170

Appendix 1: Kolathireswasthavam *175*

Appendix 2: Daiva Dasakam *181*

Appendix 3: Dharma *187*

Bibliography *188*

Foreword

Sree Narayana Guru (1856-1928), a towering figure of Indian history, is often revered as a spiritual leader, a prolific writer, and a social reformer. However, his profound insights extended far beyond the realm of spirituality. This book delves into a lesser-known facet of the thought: the economic vision of Guru.

While widely celebrated for his social reforms and spiritual teachings, Guru recognized the inextricable link between social upliftment and economic empowerment of society. He emphasized the importance of education, organization, and industry as the cornerstones of human progress. This book explores Guru's unique perspectives on topics ranging from the role of education in economic development to the importance of corporate and cooperative models, and the significance attached to the Micro, Small, and Medium Enterprises (MSMEs).

Furthermore, this work examines Guru's practical approach to the economic advancement of individuals and societies as well as the nation. He not only preached the importance of economic self-reliance but also actively encouraged his followers to get their minds engaged in productive activities. He established various institutions, including educational institutions, ashrams, and cooperatives, which served as models for economic self-sufficiency. The current work analyzes the financial and business acumen demonstrated by the Guru in establishing and managing these institutions, highlighting his innovative approaches to resource mobilization and community development.

This book builds on Sarngadharan M.'s pioneering work in Malayalam, Economic Vision of Sree Narayana Guru (2024), a seminal study that first articulated the Guru's economic insights. By translating and expanding its findings, we aim to bring the Guru's economic vision to a global audience. The word 'Beyond' is used in the title of the book to denotes 'besides' or 'apart from'.

Through insightful analysis and historical context, this work sheds light on the Guru's enduring relevance in today's rapidly changing world. This book offers valuable insights for scholars, policymakers, and anyone interested in understanding the profound impact of Guru's thought on Indian society and its potential to guide future economic and social progress.

Exploring the Guru's economic philosophy presented a unique opportunity to uncover lesser-known facets of his legacy. While primary sources were limited, our rigorous analysis of his writings, institutions, and disciples' accounts offers a comprehensive foundation for understanding his vision, with ample scope for future research. The keen interest shown in collecting the data required for the study by Dr. Retnakumari Sarngadharan, Dr. Meenakumari Sarngadharan and Abhinav Siva Ajith is thankfully appreciated. The support provided by Dr. S. Rajitha Kumar and Binod Sudarsanan was also valuable.

Sarngadharan M

Sarat Sarngadharan

1

A Blueprint for the Future: Economic Vision of the Guru

The air in the grand hall of the Central Planning Commission of India was thick with the weight of India's future. Sunlight, filtering through the imposing windows, cast long, dramatic shadows across the faces of the assembled dignitaries. Prime Minister Pandit Jawaharlal Nehru, his brow furrowed in deep contemplation, presided over the meeting, his gaze sweeping across the room with the gravity of a statesman. Beside him, Lal Bahadur Shastri, ever the pragmatist, sat attentively, his expression a blend of concern and determination. And then there was Indira Gandhi, her eyes sharp and observant, her presence commanding respect amid the seasoned leaders.

The room itself was a testament to the aspirations of the nation. Rich mahogany tables gleamed under the soft glow of the chandeliers, while portraits of national heroes adorned the walls, silent witnesses to the struggles and triumphs of a nascent nation. The then Prime Minister Rajiv Gandhi presided over the meeting in question, held in 1985, with his vision for a modern India in the computerised world.

Dr.Amartya Sen, his voice resonating with the authority of a Nobel Laureate in welfare economics, broke the silence. "Gentlemen," he began, his gaze sweeping across the assembled economists, bureaucrats, and politicians, "while our focus has rightly been on providing the necessities – food, clothing, shelter – for our people, we must now shift our gaze. True progress, I believe, lies in fortifying the social upliftment of every citizen. We must integrate factors like education, healthcare, access to income, and social security into the very framework of our economic planning."

A murmur of assent rippled through the room. Amartya Sen's words struck a chord, resonating with the deep-seated desire for a more equitable and just society. This was a progressive shift in perspective, a recognition that economic growth without social equity was a worthless victory.

Just as the consensus seemed to solidify, a voice, a touch hesitant yet firm, broke through. "If I may," began Dr. K.N. Raj, a product of Oxford University, London; a member of the Central Planning Commission since its inception in 1950 and a seasoned economist with a twinkle in his eye, "this concept of social welfare, this profound understanding of human needs, has ancient roots in our own land."

A hush fell over the room. Curiosity piqued; the assembled dignitaries turned their attention towards Raj. "I speak of Sree Narayana Guru," he continued, his voice gaining strength, "a visionary from South India, a saint who, a century ago, recognized the inextricable link between social upliftment and human flourishing."

A wave of surprise washed over the room. Sree Narayana Guru? The spiritual leader of the Ezhava community? Surely, his teachings were confined to matters of faith and spirituality! A few skeptical glances were exchanged.

Raj, sensing the skepticism, leaned forward, his voice firm yet measured. "You misunderstand," he clarified. "The Guru was not merely a spiritual guide; he was a profound social reformer, a visionary who understood the interconnectedness of social, economic, and spiritual well-being. His teachings, though often veiled in the language of spirituality, offered profound insights into the very foundations of human prosperity."

Some members exchanged skeptical glances, associating the Guru primarily with spiritual reforms for the Ezhava community. Raj, undeterred, leaned forward. 'The Guru's vision transcended caste and creed,' he said firmly. 'His economic insights, rooted in education and organization, are as relevant to India's progress as any modern theory.'

The room fell into stunned silence. No one dared to utter a word. Raj, without a word of further explanation, proceeded to expound on the Guru's philosophy. He spoke of the Sivagiri Pilgrimage, an annual gathering that transcended religious boundaries, a testament to the Guru's vision of unity and inclusivity. He described the eight themes that the Guru had outlined for the pilgrimage – themes that resonated profoundly with the very principles of social justice and economic development that the Commission was grappling with. He spoke of the Guru's emphasis on education, organization, industry, and commerce as cornerstones of human progress, highlighting their remarkable foresight in anticipating the needs of a modernizing nation.

As Raj spoke, a sense of awe descended upon the room. Here was a sage from a bygone era, a man who, a century ago, had articulated a vision of social and economic progress that resonated with the most modern of economic thinkers. His words, though delivered decades apart, seemed to echo through the hallowed halls of the Planning Commission, challenging the assembled minds to reconsider their own assumptions.

Later, during a private conversation with a young protégé, Guruvarshini, an economist of immense promise, Raj recounted the events of the meeting. "You see, Guru Varshini," he said, his voice tinged with a touch of sadness, "the world seems to have forgotten the true depth of the Guru's vision. His insights, his understanding of human needs, his emphasis on social justice – these are timeless truths, relevant even today."

Guruvarshini, intrigued by this revelation, began to delve into the Guru's writings and lectures. He was astonished to discover a wealth of economic wisdom – a profound understanding of human needs, a focus on sustainable development, and a deep-seated belief in the power of education and collective action.

The Guru, he realized, had not merely preached; he had acted. He had established educational institutions, encouraged cooperative ventures, and advocated for the economic empowerment of the marginalized. He had recognized the importance of human capital, a concept that was only beginning to gain traction in mainstream economics, long before it became a cornerstone of modern economic theory.

As Guruvarshini delved deeper, a profound realization dawned upon him: The Guru's economic vision, with its emphasis on social justice, equity, and sustainable development, was not merely relevant to the past; it was a blueprint for the future. He had anticipated the challenges of the modern world - the widening gap between the haves and the have-nots, the environmental degradation, the alienation of individuals from their communities.

The Guru, he concluded, was not just a spiritual leader; he was an economic visionary, a pioneer whose ideas, if truly understood and executed, could guide India towards a more just and prosperous future.

The meeting at the Planning Commission had planted a seed of curiosity, a seed that would blossom into a deeper exploration of the Guru's economic thought. As Guruvarshini embarked on this journey, he felt a sense of responsibility, a desire to bring the Guru's forgotten wisdom to the forefront, to share his prophetic insights with a world tussling with complex economic and social challenges.

Guruvarshini's journey mirrors the path this book undertakes: to explore the Guru's economic vision through his teachings, institutions, and disciples' legacies. In the following chapters, we delve into how his principles of unity, education, and industry offer a blueprint for modern economic empowerment.

❖ ❖ ❖

2

Building Stronger Organizations: The Guru's Vision of Unity and Collective Action

Professor Siva, a man whose presence commanded respect not through sternness but through the quiet intensity of his intellect, settled into his worn leather armchair. The afternoon sun, filtering through the dusty windows of his chamber, cast long shadows across the room, illuminating motes of dust dancing in the golden rays. His two students, Mythili and Pavan, sat opposite him, notebooks open, pens poised, anticipation etched on their faces. They knew these informal sessions with the Professor, often mentoring through history, philosophy, and economics, were far more valuable than any textbook.

"Professor," Mythili began, hesitantly, "I'm still struggling to grasp how social movements and economic development intertwine. It feels like trying to assemble a puzzle with missing pieces, especially when we talk about the financial aspects."

Professor chuckled, a warm, reassuring sound. "Ah, the grand puzzle of societal progress! It's a complex picture, I admit, and the financial dimensions add another layer of intricacy. But let's explore it together, and I promise, the picture will become clearer. Remember, economic development isn't just about cold statistics; it's about the people, their aspirations, and their collective strength, and how they leverage financial tools to achieve their aspirations."

He leaned forward, his voice gaining energy. "Let's talk about Sree Narayana Guru's vision on the topic. A name you might have encountered, but perhaps not fully appreciated."

Mythili nodded slightly. "I've heard the name, but I don't know the details."

The Professor simplified. "The Guru's impact on Kerala's social and economic fabric is immense, and his insights remain exceedingly relevant even in our time. He leveraged a fundamental truth: social progress and economic empowerment are inextricably linked, and financial inclusion plays a crucial role in that connection."

"So, how did he bridge that gap, especially the financial one?" Pavan, the other student, asked, genuinely curious.

"The Guru understood that for a society to truly prosper, all its members needed to be empowered to participate fully in the economic sphere," Professor disclosed. "He recognized that access to education, resources, and financial opportunities was essential for everyone. His call, 'Strengthen the organization,' wasn't simply about social reform; it was a strategic plan for economic advancement, including financial empowerment, for the entire society."

"Organization?" Pavan emulated. "Meaning forming groups, including financial ones?"

"Precisely!" Professor affirmed. "The Guru believed that collective action was key to unlocking economic and financial potential for everyone. He encouraged people to form associations, corporate institutions, cooperatives, and even establish business houses. He recognized that individual efforts, while valuable, were often raised through collaboration, especially when it came to accessing capital and navigating the complexities of finance. By uniting, people could pool the resources, exchange knowledge, and collectively work towards mutual financial goals."

"That makes perfect sense," Mythili said. "There's undeniable power in unity, especially when accessing loans or investment opportunities."

"Indeed," the Professor replied. "The Guru's vision extended beyond simply forming groups. He stressed the energetic importance of education, skill development, and entrepreneurship for all, including financial literacy and management skills. He wanted people to be not just laborers, but also owners, innovators, and financially shrewd individuals. He urged everyone to embrace modern technology and adapt to the ever-evolving economic and financial landscape."

The Professor paused, taking a sip of his tea. "The Guru's approach was holistic. He addressed not only the material needs of the people but also their social and spiritual well-being. He believed that genuine progress required a balanced development of all facets of human existence, including financial well-being."

"He sounds remarkably progressive for his time," Mythili commented.

"Absolutely," the Professor agreed. "Consider his views on industry. He recognized that economic growth hinged on industrial development, but he defined 'industry' expansively, encompassing agriculture, manufacturing, and services. He encouraged people to engage in trade, launch businesses, and explore emerging economic avenues. He even suggested the formation of joint-stock companies and banking institutions to facilitate economic activities, emphasizing the importance of organized finance."

"So, he was advocating for a diversified economy with a strong financial foundation?" Pavan asked.

"Exactly," the Professor confirmed. "He understood that over- dependence on a single sector could make an economy fragile, and that a lack of access to finance could stifle growth. He wanted to cultivate a resilient and dynamic economy where everyone could participate and prosper, supported by accessible and inclusive financial systems."

The Professor leaned back in his chair, his gaze thoughtful. "The Guru's ideas resonate even with contemporary economic thinkers. Consider Philip Kotler's concept of 'Marketing 3.0,' which emphasizes value-driven businesses that address societal needs. The Guru's call for ethical entrepreneurship and financial inclusion prefigures this, as seen in his support for cooperative banks financial institutions like the Cochin National Bank, which empowered marginalized communities long before modern fintech solutions like mobile banking emerged."

"It does!" Mythili exclaimed. "It's as if the Guru was articulating the same principles a century earlier, anticipating the need for financial innovation and inclusion."

"Precisely," the Professor said. "The Guru's insights into organization, education, and economic empowerment, including financial empowerment, are timeless. He acknowledged that economic development isn't simply about amassing wealth; it's about empowering individuals to be aware of their full potential, including their financial potential. It's about building a society where everyone has the opportunity to flourish, supported by robust and accessible financial systems."

"So, what key takeaways can we garner from the Guru's approach, especially concerning finance?" Pavan asked.

"Several," the Professor replied. "First, the power of collective action, including collective financial action. By organizing themselves, people can achieve far more than they could individually, especially when it comes to accessing credit, negotiating better interest rates, and pooling investment funds. Second, the importance of education and skill development, including financial literacy and management skills. Equipping people with knowledge and skills, including financial knowledge, is essential for economic advancement. Third, the need for entrepreneurship and innovation, including financial innovation. Creating new businesses and developing new products and services, including financial products and services, fuels economic growth. And finally, the importance of a holistic approach to development, including financial well-being. Addressing social, economic, and spiritual needs, along with financial needs, is crucial for creating a truly prosperous society."

"That's a lot to consider," Mythili said, feeling a sense of clarity beginning to emerge.

"Indeed," Professor agreed. "But these are fundamental principles that apply to any society, regardless of its stage of development. The Guru's legacy reminds us that economic progress is not just about technical solutions; it's about people, their aspirations, and their collective power, including their collective financial power. It's about framing a society where everyone has the opportunity to thrive, supported by inclusive and accessible financial systems."

The Professor smiled warmly. "Now, how about we delve deeper into the Guru's specific recommendations for economic development, including his vision for financial inclusion and empowerment? He had some fascinating ideas about microfinance, for example, that are still incredibly relevant today, and which anticipated many modern financial innovations."

And with that, Professor launched into a captivating discussion of the Guru's practical suggestions for economic empowerment, including his thoughts on financial instruments, cooperative banking, and access to credit, drawing parallels with modern economic theories and practices. He explored how the Guru's ideas prefigured the development of microfinance institutions, community-based lending, and other initiatives aimed at bringing financial services to underserved populations. He discussed how Guru's emphasis on education and organization was pivotal for the success of these initiatives, enabling people to manage their finances effectively and participate in the formal financial system. He also highlighted Guru's understanding of the importance of ethical financial practices and the need to protect people from exploitation.

The discussion then moved to the Guru's views on the role of technology in finance. The Professor explained how the Guru's emphasis on embracing modern technology was proactive, anticipating the rise of fintech and the digital transformation of financial services. They discussed how mobile banking, online lending platforms, and other technological innovations could help to further the Guru's vision of financial inclusion by making financial services more accessible and affordable for everybody.

The Professor also explored the Guru's ideas on the importance of savings and investment. He explained how the Guru encouraged people to save a portion of their earnings and invest wisely for their future. They discussed different investment options, from traditional savings accounts to stocks and bonds, and how the Guru's principles of financial literacy and education could help people make informed investment decisions.

The conversation then turned to the role of government in promoting financial inclusion and economic development. The Professor discussed how the Guru's ideas on organization and collective action could be applied to create strong and effective financial institutions, including cooperative banks and credit alliances. He also talked about the significance of government regulation and stewardship to ensure the stability and integrity of the financial system.

As the discussion progressed, the pieces of the puzzle were starting to fit together, revealing a clearer understanding of the intricate relationship between social movements, economic development, and financial empowerment. Guru's vision, Mythili and Pavan realized, was not just historical; it was a blueprint for a more just and prosperous future, where everyone had the opportunity to thrive, supported by inclusive and accessible financial systems. It was a vision that emphasized not just economic growth, but also financial well-being, social justice, and spiritual development. It was a holistic vision that recognized the interconnectedness of all aspects of human life and the importance of empowering individuals to reach their full potential, including their financial potential.

Sree Narayana Guru's leadership in establishing the SNDP Yogam, shaped under the provisions of the Companies Act, as a non-profit making company, in 1903, marked a pivotal moment in Indian social reform. Recognizing that true liberation required both social equality and economic self-sufficiency. The Guru's vision extended beyond caste reform to encompass economic empowerment. The SNDP Yogam, with its formal structure and legal recognition, became a model for subsequent community organizations. Its early focus on agro-industrial exhibitions and women's conferences showcased the Guru's holistic approach the development.

The Guru's economic vision was formalized in 1928 with the establishment of the Sree Narayana Dharma Sanghom, again a non-trading company under the provisions of the Companies Act. This organization aimed to promote economic activities, including trade, agriculture, handicrafts, and small-scale industries. He advocated for increased production and productivity, emphasizing the importance of creating employment opportunities exclusively under the ownership and supervision of seers. The Guru's practical approach included promoting cooperative societies, joint-stock companies, and banking institutions to strengthen economic organization. His "innovation model" was essentially an "organization initiative," demonstrating how collective action could drive both social and economic progress.

The Guru's economic pronouncements were remarkably prescient. He recognized the pervasive poverty and the crucial role of trade and commerce in societal advancement. He urged the wealthy to invest in machinery, technical know-how, and encouraged the formation of companies to overcome resource limitations. He criticized the export of raw materials and the subsequent import of finished goods, advocating for local production capabilities. He also emphasized the importance of training and education, suggesting that individuals and organizations should facilitate access to knowledge and skills.

These ideas articulated more than a century ago, remain relevant today, highlighting the Guru's deep understanding of economic principles. His focus was not on charity but on creating a system where individuals could earn a livelihood with dignity, contributing to national prosperity. His economic philosophy resonates with contemporary thinkers like Philip Kotler, who emphasizes the importance of traditional jobs, productive sectors, and fostering innovation. The Guru's emphasis on industry, encompassing agriculture, manufacturing, and services, mirrors modern economic development strategies.

The eight themes of the Sivagiri pilgrimage – education, commerce, handicrafts, organization, science and technology training, agriculture, cleanliness, and devotion to God – further illustrate the Guru's holistic vision. He recognized that true well-being encompasses physical, mental, intellectual, emotional, and spiritual happiness. The inclusion of devotion to God, grounded in his philosophy of independent spirituality, underscores the importance of ethical and moral values. His emphasis on continuous learning, practical application of knowledge, and expert lectures highlights the link between knowledge and development.

The Guru's economic philosophy was ground–breaking, focusing on empowering the oppressed through organization, education, and participation in economic activities. His approach went beyond material assistance, establishing a framework for sustainable development based on social justice and economic empowerment. His emphasis on organization extended beyond economic activities to include addressing social injustices and protecting workers' rights. The Travancore Labor Association, supported by the Guru, exemplifies his commitment to workers' rights.

The slogan "Find your friends, join the team," popularized through the newspaper 'Sahodaran' (Brother) edited by K. Ayyappan, a disciple of the Guru, further emphasizes the importance of organization in achieving social and economic goals. The Guru envisioned a society where all individuals, regardless of background, could unite for the common good. He acknowledged differing opinions but stressed the importance of resolving disputes amicably and working together. His emphasis on unity and cooperation remains relevant and reminds us of the power of collective action in achieving shared aspirations.

The Professor smiled at Pavan and Mythili. "So, you see," he said

"The Guru's economic vision is about more than just money. It is about people, empowerment, and building a better society. We have just scratched the surface – organization, education, diversification, innovation, holistic development, financial inclusion, and local production. These are key, but there is so much more to explore.

A few Commandments of the Guru require special mention. They are - Organize for Economic Power: Collective action (groups, cooperatives, business houses) amplifies individual efforts, enabling access to resources and capital.

Educate and Empower: Education (including financial literacy) empowers individuals as owners, innovators, and financially capable actors.

Diversify and Strengthen Finance: A diversified economy with accessible, inclusive financial systems is crucial for sustainable growth.

Innovate and Grow: Entrepreneurship, innovation (including financial), and technology drive economic dynamism.

Develop Holistically: Progress requires balanced material, social, intellectual, spiritual, and financial well-being.

Include Financially: Access to financial opportunities for all is essential for equitable development.

Produce Locally: Developing local production and manufacturing is key for economic self-sufficiency.

Learn and Apply: Lifelong learning and practical application of knowledge drive progress.

Act Ethically: Ethical financial practices protect individuals and ensure system integrity.

Unite and Cooperate: Collective action and cooperation are essential for shared goals.

"And that," he concluded, "is what we'll do in the successive discussions. We'll dig deeper into each of these, look at examples, and see how the Guru's wisdom still remains sustainable in the modern world. Get ready – we have got a lot to discuss."

❖ ❖ ❖

3

Conquering Poverty: The Guru's Path to Prosperity

Both Mythili and Pavan reached the Chamber of Professor Siva the next day with the intention of learning more about the economic vision of the Guru. They knew these informal sessions with the Professor often mentoring throughhistory, philosophy, and economics, were far more valuable than any textbook.

"Today," Professor began, his voice in a low rumble, "we delve into the wisdom of how to conquer poverty and achieve prosperity through the teachings of the Guru. His teachings, though rooted in a specific time and place, offer profound insights into the enduring challenges of poverty and the path to societal progress. His philosophy, while deeply spiritual, has immense practical relevance for understanding and addressing the complex socio-economic realities at the global level."

He paused, taking a sip of water from the glass on his desk. "Sree Narayana Guru's life and work were transformative. He understood that true liberation required not only social equality but also economic empowerment. As the President of India, Ram Nath Kovind opined at the Parliament, quoting the Guru, this is the ideal place 'where everyone rules as a brother, irrespective of his caste and creed.' This concept, as the Guru exhorted, emphasizes the path of brotherhood and equality for all, transcending divides."

Mythili, ever the inquisitive one, interjected, "Professor, you mentioned his teachings were spiritual. How does spirituality connect with addressing poverty?"

The Professor smiled. "That's an excellent query, Mythili. The Guru's spirituality wasn't about renouncing the world or retreating into isolation. It was about recognizing the inherent oneness of humanity. He believed that true spiritual realization was intertwined with social action. He saw the interconnectedness of all beings and understood that the well-being of the individual was inseparable from the well-being of society. His spiritual framework provided the ethical foundation for his social and economic activism. He offered an 'independent spirituality as an alternative to the usual religion-based spirituality,' which is a decisive distinction."

Mythili interjected, 'Like the SNDP Yogam he founded?'

'Exactly,' Professor replied. 'In 1903, the Guru established the SNDP Yogam as a non-profit under the Companies Act, uniting communities to advocate for education and economic opportunities.'

Pavan, always more inclined towards practical applications, asked, "So, what were the Guru's specific ideas on tackling poverty?"

"The Guru's approach was multifaceted," Professor replied. "He recognized that poverty wasn't simply a dearth of material resources. It was a complex issue with intellectual, physical, and emotional dimensions. He identified three key problems that contributed to poverty: hunger, timidity, and lack of intellectual ability. He saw these as interconnected, each reinforcing the others. He framed these as problems of the stomach (hunger), the body (timidity), and the head (intellectual ability). He stressed that each individual should strive to solve these problems one by one."

Stomach (Hunger): Lack of food, hindering physical and mental development.

Body (Timidity): Lack of self-confidence often stems from powerlessness.

Head (Intellectual Ability): Limited access to education and opportunities, trapping individuals in poverty.

He picked up a piece of chalk and began writing on the small whiteboard behind him. "Think about it. Hunger, the most basic need, affects physical and mental well-being. A person who is constantly worried about where their next meal will come from can hardly focus on education or personal development. This leads to a sense of powerlessness, what the Guru called 'timidity' – a lack of self-confidence. And without education and opportunities for intellectual growth, individuals are trapped in a cycle of poverty. This is what he meant when he spoke of the 'three problems with poverty.' He asked, 'Is there anything more than that?' He understood that these three combined create a 'great misery.'"

Mythili nodded. "It's like a vicious cycle. Each problem feeds into the others."

"Exactly," the Professor agreed. "The Guru understood this interconnectedness and emphasized the importance of addressing all three aspects. He believed that education, organization, and industry were the keys to breaking this cycle. His famous call to action was: 'Become independent through education, become strong through organization, become prosperous through industrialization.' This wasn't merely a slogan; it was a comprehensive master plan for social and economic transformation."

Pavan scribbled the quote in his notebook. "That's a powerful statement. It's indeed action-oriented."

"Indeed, it is," the Professor said. "The Guru wasn't just a philosopher; he was a pragmatist. He believed in translating his ideas into concrete action. He understood the crucial role of 'intellectual ability', which could be improved through education. He saw education as the foundation for intellectual development, which in turn fueled economic progress. He recognized that education empowers individuals to think critically, solve problems, and adapt to changing circumstances. It opens new opportunities and breaks down barriers induced by ignorance and inclination. As he stated, 'Education is important. This will bring wealth and prosperity.' "

The Professor turned back to the whiteboard and wrote:

Education → Intellectual Development → Economic Progress.

"But education alone isn't enough," he continued. The Guru also emphasized the importance of organization. He understood that individuals working together could achieve far more than they could alone. The Organization provides a platform for collective action, allowing marginalized communities to voice their concerns, advocate for their rights, and assemble their resources. It fosters a sense of solidarity and empowers individuals to challenge systemic inequalities. He stressed the need to 'unite and become strong,' a call that resonates even today. The Guru's call to 'unite and become strong' resonates with collective action principles in modern social movements, such as trade unions. Unlike Karl Marx's focus on class struggle in industrialized Europe, the Guru addressed India's caste-based inequalities, advocating organization to empower marginalized communities economically and socially. Karl Marx also viewed that the Indian society was caste-ridden and class-ridden.

The Professor added to the whiteboard: Organization → Collective Action → Empowerment.

"And finally," the Professor said, "the Guru reinforced the importance of industry. By 'industry,' he meant productive economic activities that generate wealth and create job opportunities. He encouraged individuals to engage in entrepreneurship, develop new skills, and contribute to the economic growth of their communities. He believed that economic independence was essential for true freedom and self-respect. He urged people to 'achieve prosperity through industry.' He recognized that 'you are all money,' meaning everyone has the potential to generate wealth through their work. He lamented that much of this potential was wasted, citing examples like excessive drinking, and emphasized the need for prudent management of funds."

Professor slanted back in his chair, his gaze drifting towards the window. "The Guru's teachings also offer valuable insights for individuals. He encouraged everyone to take responsibility for their own development. He believed that each individual has the potential to overcome challenges and achieve their full potential. He emphasized the importance of self-reliance, hard work, and perseverance. He stimulated individuals to acquire extra skills, embrace lifelong learning, and contribute to the betterment of their communities. He recognized that some will have more money, education, hygiene, etc. For others, it may be less.

He stressed that the shortage of money and education were the primary challenges, and that addressing these was crucial. He famously declared, 'It's not true that you don't have money. You are all money.' This wasn't just a philosophical statement; it was a call to comprehend the inherent potential within each individual. He urged people to utilize their skills and talents to generate wealth and improve their lives. He also cautioned against wasteful spending, particularly citing the example of excessive consumption of alcohol, focusing on the importance of financial responsibility."

Mythili asked, "Professor, you mentioned that the Guru's philosophy has influenced modern development programs. Can you give us some specific examples?"

"Certainly," the Professor replied. "One example is the concept of microfinance. The Guru's idea of families contributing to a common fund for education prefigures microfinance, as seen in his support for cooperative societies. For example, the SNDP Yogam facilitated community-driven savings schemes, akin to modern microfinance institutions like Grameen Bank, which provide small loans to empower women and rural communities. Microfinance provides small loans to individuals and communities, particularly women, who lack access to traditional banking services. These loans can be used to start businesses, improve livelihoods, and empower individuals to break free from poverty. This idea of collective contribution for a common objective is central to many of the Guru's teachings. He understood the power of pooling resources to achieve larger goals."

Pavan added, "I remember reading about Muhammad Yunus, who won the Nobel Peace Prize for his work in microfinance. His Grameen Bank has helped millions of people around the world to escape from poverty." He is currently the chief advisor of the interim Government of Bangladesh.

"Exactly," the Professor confirmed. "Yunus's work is a testament to the power of microfinance. Another example is the emphasis on education and skills development in many poverty reduction programmes. The Guru's precept that education is the key to economic empowerment has been widely lauded and integrated into development strategies around the world. Many programmes focus on providing access to education and vocational training, particularly for marginalized communities. These programmes aim to equip individuals with the skills and knowledge they need to participate in the workforce and improve their livelihoods. Guru's vision is clearly reflected in the modern understanding of development, which values human capital development as a paramount ignite of economic growth."

He paused, then added, "It's important to remember that the Guru's vision was not just about economic development. It was about holistic development – the development of the individual and the community." He believed that true progress requires not only economic empowerment but also social and spiritual transformation. He magnified the importance of ethical conduct, compassion, and social responsibility. He believed that individuals should not only strive for their own well-being but also volunteer for the well-being of others. He beheld that 'poverty not eradicated, far away,' emphasizing the urgency of addressing this issue.

The prayer scribbled by the guru for the use of the common people goes like this:

'Poverty's great misery, may it never afflict me,

May deluded ego stay far away,

May good fortune come to me to stay close to kind people,

O! Supreme Lord, reigning in the temple of Kolathukara.'

Mythili asked, "the Professor, how did Guru's own life reflect on his teachings?"

"Guru's life was a living example of his philosophy," Professor replied. "He devoted his life to serving others, particularly the marginalized and oppressed. He challenged the rigid social structures of his time and advocated for equality and justice. He established schools, temples, and other industrial and service organizations to empower communities and promote social reforms. He understood that merely stating the principle wasn't enough; it needed to be actively administered through social and economic reforms. His address on the first anniversary of the Aruvippuram consecration, where he discussed the 'three problems of poverty,' illustrates his commitment to connecting spiritual principles with concrete action. He used the occasion to engage with the community, asking them directly about their most pressing concerns, which revealed poverty as the primary challenge. He then proceeded to dissect the issue into its core components – hunger, cowardice, and lack of intellectual ability – offering a framework for addressing it."

He continued, "The Guru's work extended beyond spiritual proclamation. He was deeply compared with the material well-being of individuals and communities. He recognized that social and economic factors were intertwined and that addressing one without the other would be ineffective. He understood that, 'as the social and economic factors progress, natural progress in the cultural, political, and legal spheres can be accomplished by the masses.

"The Guru's address in 1920, where he reinforced the importance of education and financial responsibility, is a testament to his practical approach. He didn't just talk about poverty; he offered concrete solutions and strategies for overcoming it. He concealed the existing differences in wealth, education, and other factors, but he emphasized the fundamental unity of humankind. He saw education as the key to unlocking individual potential and achieving prosperity. He urged people to invest in education, recognizing its transformative power. He also stressed the significance of financial prudence, urging people to avoid wasteful spending and invest wisely."

Mythili asked, "Professor, you mentioned the eight themes proposed for the Sivagiri Pilgrimage. What were those, and what was their significance?"

"The eight themes proposed for the Sivagiri pilgrimage outline the Guru's comprehensive vision for social and economic development," the Professor replied. "They are: education, cleanliness, godliness, organization, agriculture, commerce, handicrafts, and technical training in that order. These themes were not just abstract ideas; they were practical areas of focus for community development. The Guru emphasized the importance of inviting experts in each of these fields to share their knowledge and insights with the pilgrims. He motivated people not just to listen but also to put what they learned into practice. He believed that this continuous learning and practical application were essential for individual and societal progress. He stressed that development should not be limited to any one community but should benefit all. He envisioned a society where everyone had the opportunity to thrive. It's noteworthy that the Guru placed education as the first among these eight themes, underscoring its paramount importance. His vision aligns with modern economic thinking, which recognizes human capital as a crucial driver of economic growth. Comparing these themes with the seven essential elements for a civilized nation – food, shelter, education, health, income, and social security – reveals the remarkable foresight of Guru's vision. He was addressing the fundamental needs of individuals and communities long before these concepts became widely recognized by the economists and policymakers."

Pavan asked, "Professor, you also mentioned the *Kolathiresasthavam*. What was that?"

"The *Kolathiresasthavam* was a composition by the Guru for meditation and bhajan," the Professor explained. "It was given to devotees during His second *Shiva Prathishta at Kolathukara* at Thiruvananthapuram, Kerala in 1893. In its ten verses, The Guru addressed the needs of ordinary devotees, including the removal of disease, poverty, and ignorance. The prayer includes the expression 'Garibi Mahaduhakham,' highlighting the great suffering caused by poverty. This underscores the Guru's deep compassion for the poor and his commitment to alleviating their suffering. It validated that his concern for the material well-being of individuals was an integral part of his spiritual vision."

Pavan came up with a new piece of information at this stage. "I have read in a book that Abhijit Vinayak Banerjee, the US economist who is engaged in evolving and executing poverty alleviation strategies, shared the Nobel Prize. Economics in 2019 with his better half, Esther Duflo, and his colleague, Michael Kremer. Nobel Prize was awarded to them 'for their experimental approach to alleviating global poverty'. It needs special mention that Abhijit was born and brought up in India. Abhijit and Esther became the sixth couple to jointly win Noble Prize. Has this information got any relevance in our current discussion?"

"Certainly," the Professor said. "The Guru taught us the significance of poverty alleviation more than a century ago. Besides, this is a classic example of citing the farsightedness of the Guru on global issues."

The Guru's economic vision was comprehensive and forward-looking. He recognized the interconnectedness of education, organization, and industry, and he understood the importance of addressing the root causes of poverty. His teachings remain relevant even today, offering valuable insights for individuals, communities, and policymakers striving to create a more just and equitable world. He understood that 'education is essential for economic development,' and that 'organization is as necessary for economic activity as it is for the spread of education.' These principles are as valid today as they were a century ago. His emphasis on 'industry,' meaning productive economic activity, highlights the importance of creating opportunities for individuals to earn a livelihood and contribute to the economic growth of their communities. He believed that true prosperity could only be achieved through a combination of intellectual development, social organization, and economic activity.

His foresight is also evident in his understanding of the psychological and emotional dimensions of poverty. He comprehended that poverty can lead to a sense of powerlessness and 'cowardice,' which can further perpetuate the cycle of poverty. His emphasis on education and organization was not just about economic empowerment; it was also about building self-confidence. He believed that individuals who are educated and organized are better equipped to challenge injustice and advocate for their rights. His teachings empower individuals to take control of their lives and become agents of change in their communities. He perceived that 'improvement of intellectual ability through education' was crucial not only for economic advancement but also for personal growth and social empowerment.

The Guru's influence extends beyond specific programs and initiatives. His philosophy has shaped the way we think about development and social change. He outlined the importance of holistic development, recognizing that human well-being encompasses physical, mental, emotional, intellectual, and spiritual dimensions. His teachings remind us that true progress requires not only economic growth but also social justice, environmental sustainability, and ethical conduct. He believed that 'life should be an example,' emphasizing the importance of living a life of integrity and service. He believed that individuals should strive not only for their own well-being but also for the well-being of others. His life and teachings serve as a powerful reminder of the interconnectedness of all beings and the importance of compassion and social responsibility.

His understanding of the human condition is remarkably insightful. "The 'Management Gurus' of modern times have suggested some observations and practical methods similar to those of the Guru", highlighting the enduring relevance of his philosophy. He anticipated modern management theories that emphasize the importance of holistic well-being for productivity and success. He understood that individuals need physical, mental, emotional, intellectual, and spiritual comfort to engage fully in economic activities. His teachings offer a holistic framework for personal and professional development, highlighting the importance of balance and integration.

The Guru's legacy is not just about the past; it is also about the future. His teachings offer timeless wisdom that can guide us in addressing the challenges of the 21st century. His emphasis on education, organization, and industry remains as relevant today as it was a century ago. His holistic approach to development, which considers the intellectual, physical, emotional, and spiritual dimensions of human well-being, is even more important in a world facing complex and interlinked challenges. His life and teachings serve as an inspiration for those working to create a more just, equitable, and sustainable world. His message of equality, brotherhood, and social responsibility continues to resonate with people across cultures and generations. His wisdom is a valuable resource for navigating the complexities of our time and building a better future for all.

The Professor paused, looking at his two students. "The Guru's life and teachings offer a rich tapestry of wisdom," he concluded. "He was not just a philosopher; he was a social reformer, an educator, an organizer, and a visionary leader. The contributions to social and economic development are immeasurable. His legacy continues as the Guru to inspire and empower individuals and communities around the world. His teachings offer a timeless message of hope, equality, and social justice. By studying his life and philosophy, we can gain valuable insights into the challenges we face today and find inspiration for building a better tomorrow."

Mythili and Pavan, their notebooks filled with notes and their minds buzzing with new ideas, looked at the Professor with renewed respect. They had embarked on a journey through the wisdom of Sree Narayana Guru, and they knew that this journey would continue to shape their understanding of the world and their role in it. They had learned not just about the past but also about the present and the future. They had discovered the enduring relevance of the Guru's teachings and the power of his vision to inspire positive changes. As they left Professor from his chamber, they carried with them not just notes and quotes but also a renewed sense of purpose and a deeper understanding of the interconnectedness of all beings. They knew that the wisdom of Sree Narayana Guru would continue to guide them on their own paths towards creating a more just and equitable world.

The key points of the discussions held were summarized by Pavan as stated below:

- **Poverty's Triple Threat:** Hunger, lack of self-confidence ("cowardice"), and limited intellectual ability (due to lack of education) are interconnected and perpetuate poverty.
- **Education Empowers:** Education is foundational for intellectual development, driving economic progress and opening opportunities.
- **Organization Amplifies:** Collective action through organization empowers communities to address inequalities and achieve shared goals.
- **Industry Creates Prosperity:** Productive economic activities, entrepreneurship, and skill development are essential for wealth generation and opportunity creation.
- **Holistic Development is the Key:** True progress requires economic, social, and spiritual transformation, including ethical conduct and social responsibility.
- **Self-Reliance and Action:** Individuals must embrace self-reliance, lifelong learning, and contribute actively to their communities.
- **Collective Goals:** Small, shared contributions for common goals (e.g., education) foreshadow microfinance principles.

- **Practical Focus:** The Guru's teachings emphasize practical application through initiatives like the eight Sivagiri pilgrimage themes.
- **Financial Prudence Matters:** Responsible financial management, avoiding wasteful spending, is crucial for economic well-being.

❖ ❖ ❖

4

Education as Wealth, Service as Purpose: The Guru's Vision

"Mythili, Pavan, come in," Professor Siva called out, gesturing towards the chairs in his chamber. "Today, we need to talk over something quite erudite – the Guru's philosophy and its relevance to education, particularly in light of recent events."

Mythili and Pavan settled in, notebooks open. "We were reading about the Andhra Pradesh Deputy Chief Minister's speech, sir," Mythili began. "He mentioned the Guru's highlight on education leading to independence and an empowered society."

"Precisely," Professor nodded. "And it's not just him. Remember another Deputy Chief Minister of Andhra Pradesh, In 2025, The Chief Minister of Kerala praised the Guru's educational legacy during a state education conference, reflecting his enduring influence on policy. These are not isolated episodes. They ignited Guru's immortal influence."

Pavan chimed in, "It's remarkable how the education system in Kerala is often cited as a model. High literacy, free education, social justice – it all seems to connect back to you, the Guru's call for '***Become Independent with Education***' in the early 20th century."

"Absolutely," the Professor agreed. "Progress of Kerala is a testament to the power of that vision. Think about the social context of the time. Over 75 per cent of the population faced severe discrimination, denied access to education, employment, and even basic freedoms during the previous century. Guru recognized that education was the key to breaking these chains."

Mythili added, "It's like he understood that education is the foundation for overcoming all kinds of barriers – your background, gender inequality, poverty. It's the most powerful tool for empowerment, especially for women."

"Exactly," Professor affirmed. "And that understanding is more relevant than ever. In our globalized world, education is vital for human capital development, driving economic growth, and creating opportunities. The Guru's farsightedness was undeniably outstanding."

"But sir," Pavan inquired, "what makes the Guru so special, beyond his emphasis on education?"

The Professor leaned forward. "His approach was holistic. For 40 years, he tirelessly championed acquiring knowledge, starting with 'Vidya' – independence through education – and then expanding to 'Wealth will become Vidya; Vidya will become Seva' – knowledge leading to service."

"He did not just talk," Mythili observed. "He established Sanskrit schools, supported English language learning, and encouraged those who could afford it to send bright students abroad."

"Indeed," the Professor said. "He understood the magnitude of both traditional learning and embracing new opportunities. He even advised against excessive temple construction, suggesting that educational institutions should be the priority. He saw temples as potentially divisive, while education could unite people."

Pavan noted, "It seems like his educational plan was quite comprehensive, covering everything from access for all, to girls' education, the importance of English, scientific and technical training, and even financial assistance for the students."

"Perfectly," Professor confirmed. "And his answer to Mahatma Gandhi in 1925, when asked about solving the problems of the downtrodden, was simple yet profound: 'They should have education and wealth.' He recognized the interconnectedness of the two components."

Mythili recalled, "You mentioned the Sivagiri Pilgrimage, Professor. How does that tie into his educational philosophy?"

"The Guru envisioned the pilgrimage not just as a religious ritual, but as an opportunity for learning and development," the Professor explained. "He outlined specific themes for lectures and discussions – education, cleanliness, devotion to God, organization, agriculture, trade, handicrafts, and technical subjects. He wanted people to listen, learn, and then put that knowledge into practice."

"So, it was about practical application, not just theoretical understanding," Pavan summarized.

"Exactly," the Professor said. "The Guru defined 'Vidya' as expert knowledge, including technical and scientific skills. He emphasized the importance of attention, a firm belief in one's ability, and deep thinking. He believed that combining these elements would make everyone's work more effective."

"It's fascinating how his ideas reverberate even today," Mythili commented. "With the rise of online learning, the knowledge economy, and Science, Technology, Engineering and Mathematics (STEM) and Science,

Technology, Engineering, Arts and Mathematics (STEAM) education, it feels like we're building on the foundation he laid."

The Professor nodded. "The world has changed amazingly, with cost-effective online education, readily available resources, and a focus on visual and auditory learning. The 'knowledge economy' has become a driving force, with innovation and creativity playing a supreme role. Even artificial intelligence and other technologies are shaping education."

Pavan added, "And the emphasis on 'knowledge capital' – recognizing knowledge as a pivotal factor of production – feels like a direct extension of the Guru's vision."

"It is," the Professor said. "The Kasturi Rangan Commission appointed by the Government of India (2019), in its report, also highlights the need to integrate these innovative resources into the school curriculum, a modern echo of the Guru's century-old advocacy for practical, accessible, and inclusive education that adapts to the needs of the time. We're moving towards a world where knowledge is a commodity, driving economic development and shaping global dynamics."

"So, what's the takeaway, Professor?" Mythili asked.

"The Guru's message is timeless," Professor concluded. "Education is not just about acquiring information; it's about empowerment, social transformation, and building a better future. It's about fostering critical thinking, problem-solving skills, and a spirit of service. And as we navigate the complexities of the 21st century, his vision remains a guiding light."

Key learnings from today's discussions were condensed by Pavan as:

- **Education = Liberation:** The Guru embraced education as the path to individual and social freedom, especially for the marginalized.

- **Knowledge + Action = Service:** He deduced that knowledge ("Vidya") should lead to wealth creation and, ultimately, service ("Seva") to society.
- **Holistic Education:** The Guru patronized for a balanced education, combining traditional learning with modern skills and sciences.
- **Practical Wisdom:** He magnified applying knowledge practically for individual and societal improvement.
- **Timeless Vision:** The Guru's focus on education for empowerment and progress remains relevant in today's knowledge-driven world.

❖ ❖ ❖

5

Igniting Industry: A Call to Action

"Mythili, Pavan, come in, come in," Professor Siva gestured towards the worn leather chairs in his chamber. Sunlight streamed through the tall windows, illuminating dust motes dancing in the air. "Today, we excavate into a fascinating phase - the Guru's vision for industrialization."

Mythili, ever the diligent student, already had her notebook open. "Professor, we've read the excerpts. It's inspiring how the Guru connected spiritual principles with economic progress."

Pavan, more inclined towards practical application, chimed in, "But Sir, the concept of 'industry' seems much broader than just factories. The text talks about agriculture, manufacturing, services, it's almost everything!"

The Professor smiled. "Precisely, Pavan. That's the brilliance of the Guru's foresight. Let's start with the core idea. The Upanishads and the Bible, as you know, both caution against the infatuation with wealth. Yet, as Swami Vivekananda eloquently put it, 'God appears in the form of bread before the hungry.' The Guru understood this delicate perspective. He recognized that material prosperity is imperative for overall well-being – physical, mental, intellectual, emotional, and spiritual."

"So, it's not about rejecting material pursuit altogether," Mythili offered, "but finding a balance, using wealth as a means to a greater end?"

"Exactly," the Professor affirmed. "The Guru believed that happiness, the ultimate goal, is more readily attained when individuals and communities are prosperous. He reinforced the magnitude of organized efforts, education, and, crucially, industry, for societal evolution. And he placed industry right after education in his priorities."

"But why industry?" Pavan asked. "Couldn't they have focused solely on agriculture, given the predominantly agrarian society at the time?"

"The Guru's vision extended beyond that," the Professor explained. "He understood that 'industry' encompasses far more than just manufacturing. While the common understanding at the time equated 'industry' with production, the Guru's perspective was strikingly prescient. He saw it as any economic activity across all sectors – agriculture, manufacturing, *and* services – that contributes to wellness through the efficient, skilled, and impactful use of resources."

He picked up a piece of chalk and drew a Venn diagram on the blackboard. "Think of it like this. Plantation industries fall under agriculture, fertilizer production under manufacturing, and banking or tourism under services. Industry, in the Guru's view, is the overarching principle of generating returns on investment through the rational and scientific use of human and material resources."

Mythili pondered this. "So, a farmer adopting better irrigation techniques, a craftsman improving his skills, or even a local community setting up a cooperative bank – all these could be considered as contributing to 'industry' in this broader sense?"

"Absolutely," the Professor nodded. "It took nearly a century for this comprehensive understanding of 'industry' to become widely accepted.

The Guru was a visionary. Even in his time, his instructions to the SNDP Yogam speakers emphasized agriculture, handicrafts, trade, and technical training *within* the context of industry. He wanted them to explore how these sectors could flourish, demonstrating his integrated approach."

Pavan, ever practical, asked, "But Sir, how did the Guru go about implementing this vision? Just talking about it wouldn't be enough, surely."

"Indeed," Professor agreed. "The Guru wasn't just about pronouncements. He was a man of action. He recognized that the first step was creating awareness. He initiated a systematic campaign to educate the people about the importance of industry in achieving prosperity. He truly pioneered the concept of awareness for industrialization."

"What kind of awareness campaigns did he organize?" Mythili inquired.

"The SNDP Yogam, under the Guru's guidance, made industrialization a central objective. They organized lectures across the country, highlighting the need for industry. But the Guru went further. He introduced something quite revolutionary for the time – agricultural and industrial exhibitions."

Pavan's eyes widened. "Exhibitions? Like trade fairs?"

"Precisely," Professor confirmed. "The first such exhibition was held in connection with the second annual conference of the SNDP Yogam at Kollam in 1905. It was a groundbreaking initiative, supported even by the Maharaja of Travancore and the British Rulers. Dr.Palpu, in his presidential address, as the exhibition committee chairman, pinpointed the value of such events in fostering a competitive spirit and driving overall progress."

"So, it was about showcasing products and inspiring people?" Mythili asked.

"Exactly. It was about demonstrating the potential of industry, triggering curiosity, and encouraging communities to explore new avenues for economic activities. The second exhibition, held at Kannur in 1907, was even more dynamic. They observed a few organizational deficiencies experienced in the exhibition of Kollam and organized the second one meticulously."

The Professor paused, picking up a copy of *Vivekodayam* magazine. "This report from the Kannur exhibition, edited by Kumaran Asan, the General Secretary of the SNDP Yogam and a Great poet, highlights the key objectives: generating curiosity, digesting knowledge, comparing products, understanding new machines and methods, and observing breakthroughs in handicrafts. They even managed to bring in products from neighboring countries like Burma and Ceylon, making it a truly international event! And the government supported the initiative by offering discounted train fares for both transportation of goods and travel of visitors."

He read a passage from the magazine. "The exhibition was considered as a guide to understand the seasonal changes in the production processes in the agricultural and industrial sectors.' It wasn't just a festival; it was an educational experience."

"It sounds like a massive undertaking," Pavan commented. "Organizing something like that in those times must have been incredibly challenging."

"It was," the Professor acknowledged. "But the Guru's vision and the dedication of his followers made it possible. The inaugural speech by Castle Stuart, the deputy of a British General and a prominent figure in the Madras Presidency, praised the exhibition for showcasing the diverse products from various communities and regions, and for providing a platform for comparison and erudition. He even acknowledged that this exhibition was more rewarding than the one held in Kollam."

"So, these exhibitions were a cardinal part of Guru's strategy to promote industrialization," Mythili summarized.

"Absolutely," the Professor replied. "They were a powerful tool for rearing awareness, inspiring innovation, and fostering a spirit of enterprise. But it's crucial to understand that these exhibitions were just one piece of the puzzle. Guru's vision for industrialization was multifaceted."

He leaned back in his chair. "He believed that industrialization was the path to economic progress for individuals, communities, and the nation as a whole. He advocated for the use of modern science, technology, and machinery, even suggesting importing them from abroad if necessary. He encouraged joint ventures for those who lacked the resources to start enterprises individually. He highlighted the importance of educating children in the scientific processing of raw materials and transforming them into innovative products. He even proposed sending young people to developed countries for advanced training and bringing back their expertise to share with others."

"That's quite comprehensive," Pavan remarked. "It covers everything from infrastructure to education to international collaboration."

"Indeed," Professor agreed. "And the Guru also stressed the significance of continuous awareness campaigns and adapting traditional handicrafts to modern demands. Crucially, he insisted that all economic activities, including industrialization, must be grounded in human values and moral principles. Profit should not be pursued at the expense of ethical considerations."

"So, the Guru's vision was not just about economic growth," Mythili observed, "but also about social and ethical development."

"Precisely," Professor affirmed. "He understood that true progress encompasses all these dimensions. Now, to fully appreciate the impact of

Guru's initiatives, we need to examine the specific programs he devised and implemented to assess their influence on society. That will be the focus of our next discussion." He smiled at his students. "This is a rich and complex topic, and I'm glad you're both engaging with it so thoughtfully. We must understand the Guru's vision and its relevance even today."

The summary of the current discussions

- **Holistic Development:** The Guru's concept of 'industry' encompassed all economic activities (agriculture, manufacturing, services) aimed at prosperity through efficient resource use. It was not just about factories, but a broader principle of generating fair returns on investment.
- **Balance:** He advocated for material prosperity to achieve greater well-being (physical, mental, intellectual, emotional, and spiritual), not as an end.
- **Awareness for Industrialization:** The Guru pioneered awareness campaigns to educate people about the importance of industry for individual and societal progress.
- **Industrial Exhibitions:** He initiated agricultural and industrial exhibitions to showcase products, inspire innovation, and encourage communities to explore new economic avenues. These exhibitions served as educational experiences, promoting knowledge sharing and competition.
- **Comprehensive Approach:** The Guru's vision included modernizing methods, utilizing technology, promoting joint ventures, emphasizing education (especially in scientific processing of raw materials), international collaboration, and adapting traditional skills.
- **Ethical Foundation:** The Guru stressed that all economic activities, including industrialization, must be grounded in human values and moral principles. He firmly believed that profit must never be pursued at the expense of ethical considerations.

❖ ❖ ❖

6

UNLOCKING GROWTH: THE POWER OF MICRO, SMALL, AND MEDIUM ENTERPRISES FOR ECONOMIC GROWTH

"Good morning! Mythili, Pavan,' Professor Siva began, his voice resonating in the quiet chamber, 'today we'll delve into the practical application of economic vision – the creation of wealth through enterprise."

Mythili, ever the keen observer, noted, "Professor, the text mentions two types of economies – resource abundant and wealth abundant. Guru seemed to favor the latter. Why? "An Excellent question, Mythili," the Professor replied. "The Guru believed in leveraging resource abundance to create wealth abundance. He visualized a society where resources were utilized through labor and ingenuity to generate prosperity for all. It's about making the two reciprocals for sustainable development."

Pavan, always eager to understand the mechanics, interjected, "So, it's not just about having resources, but about actively transforming them into something valuable?"

"Precisely, Pavan," the Professor affirmed. "And this is where the Guru's three commandments become crucial: 'Become independent through education,' 'Become strong through organization,' and 'Achieve wealth through industry.' These are interconnected principles. Education fosters knowledge, and that leads to organizational consciousness. And when these combine with industry, you have job creation and stable income. It's a timeless model for development."

"It makes sense," Mythili ruminated "Knowledge empowers individuals, organization amplifies their impact, and industry provides the means for economic advancement."

"Right," the Professor agreed. "The Guru articulated this principle over a century ago. He understood that true progress requires a holistic approach, where individuals are empowered to contribute to the economic well-being of the community."

Pavan, ever the pragmatist, asked, "But Sir, how did the Guru translate this vision into action? What specific steps did he take to encourage enterprise?"

"The Guru recognized the need for a multi-pronged approach," the Professor explained. "He started by promoting social awareness about the importance of industrialization. He organized industrial exhibitions and lectures by experts to showcase opportunities and inspire individuals. This was the first phase – creating the spark of entrepreneurial spirit."

"Like the exhibitions we discussed earlier?" Mythili inquired.

"Precisely," Professor confirmed. "Those exhibitions weren't just about showcasing products; they were about igniting the desire for economic participation. The second phase involved encouraging individuals to start their enterprises. The Guru understood that individual initiative is crucial for economic growth."

"But what about those who lacked the resources or the confidence to start on their own?" Pavan asked.

"That's where the Guru's foresight truly shines," the Professor explained. "He encouraged the formation of joint-stock companies and mutual aid cooperative societies. He understood that collective effort could overcome individual limitations. By clustering resources and expertise, communities could achieve what individuals couldn't."

"So, it was about nurturing both individual and collective entrepreneurship?" Mythili summarized.

"Exactly," the Professor replied. "And the third phase, perhaps the most crucial, involved developing a Dharma-based management style. The Guru believed that enterprises should not only be profitable but also ethical and socially responsible. He emphasized values and principles in business operations."

Pavan, intrigued, asked, "Dharma-based management? What does that embrace?"

"It's a holistic approach," the Professor explained, "where ethical considerations, social responsibility, and community well-being are integrated into business practices. It's about creating a sustainable and equitable economic system."

Mythili observed, "It's interesting how the Guru's vision aligns with modern concepts of corporate social responsibility and stakeholder capitalism."

"Indeed," Professor agreed. "The Guru's ideas were far ahead of their time. He recognized that businesses have a responsibility to contribute to the overall well-being of society, not just to maximize profits."

Pavan, always focused on practical implications, asked, "Sir, what about the Micro, Small, and Medium Enterprises – MSMEs? The text mentions the Guru's contribution to this sector."

"Ah, yes," Professor said, a hint of frustration in his voice. "The Guru's pioneering work in this area is often overlooked. He conceptualized and implemented the principles of MSMEs long before the term became widely recognized. Surprisingly, this fact hasn't received more attention from economists and planners."

He paused, picking up a book from his desk. "Even Dr. K. N. Raj, a renowned economist, mentioned the Guru's contribution in the 1980s, but it hasn't led to substantial research or acknowledgment. It's rather unfortunate, especially considering the crucial role MSMEs play in the economy today."

"So, Guru's ideas predate the current understanding of MSMEs?" Mythili asked.

"Absolutely," the Professor confirmed. "He understood the importance of small and medium-sized enterprises in generating employment, driving innovation, and promoting inclusive growth. He laid the groundwork for the development of this sector in India."

Pavan, ever curious, asked, "Professor, can you give us some statistics about MSMEs in India today?"

"Certainly, Pavan," the Professor responded. "The MSME sector contributes roughly 15 percent to India's GDP. As of October 2021, approximately 11 million MSMEs were operating in India, employing over 111 million people. These numbers highlight the significant role MSMEs play in the Indian economy."

Mythili, reflecting on the discussion, remarked, "It's remarkable how the Guru's vision, conceived over a century ago, continues to be relevant today. His emphasis on education, organization, and industry, combined with ethical considerations, provides a solid foundation for sustainable economic development."

"Indeed," Professor affirmed. "The Guru's legacy extends far beyond spiritual matters. His economic insights are just as profound and impactful. He understood the interconnectedness of social, economic, and ethical progress. And his work serves as a guiding light for building a more just and prosperous society."

Mythili and Pavan summarized the lessons they learned for the day as stated below:

- **Resource Abundance vs Wealth Abundance:** The Guru advocated for transforming resource abundance into wealth abundance through labor and ingenuity, emphasizing value addition for sustainable development.
- **Three Commandments of the Guru:** These principles - "Become independent through education," "Become strong through organization," and "Achieve wealth through the industry" - are interconnected. Education empowers, organization amplifies impact, and industry provides economic means.
- **Multi-Pronged Approach to Enterprise:** The Guru promoted social awareness about industrialization, prompted individual enterprises, and advocated collective entrepreneurship through joint-stock companies and cooperatives.
- **Dharma-Based Management:** He believed in ethical, socially responsible businesses that consider community well-being alongside

profitability, aligning with modern concepts of corporate social responsibility.

- **Pioneering MSME Concept:** The Guru conceptualized and implemented the principles of micro, small, and medium enterprises (MSMEs) long before the term was widely recognized, emphasizing their importance for employment, innovation, and inclusive growth.

❖ ❖ ❖

7

The Art of Management: Leadership Lessons from the Guru

Professor Siva adjusted his spectacles and looked at Mythili and Pavan. "Today, we'll explore another facet of the Guru's multifaceted vision – his insights on Dharma and its application in management, particularly within the context of industry."

Mythili, ever the observant student, began, "Professor, the text mentions a growing emphasis on Science, Technology, Engineering, and Mathematics (STEM) subjects in higher education, but also a parallel trend towards compulsory studies in humanities and social sciences. Why this multidisciplinary approach?"

"Excellent point, Mythili," the Professor responded. "The world is changing rapidly, driven by scientific and technological advancements. We need specialists in the STEM fields to innovate and drive economic growth. However, we also need individuals with a strong understanding of social, cultural, and ethical dimensions. A multidisciplinary approach ensures that scientists and technical experts are not isolated in their fields, and that those in the humanities and social sciences have a basic understanding of scientific principles. It's about creating well-rounded individuals who can navigate the complexities of the modern world." *This highlights the leadership lesson of* ***anticipating future needs and fostering holistic development*** *in individuals and organizations.* Leaders must recognize the interconnectedness of different fields and encourage cross-disciplinary thinking to solve complex problems.

Pavan, always keen to understand the practical implications, asked, "And what about the discussion on management styles? The text mentions a need for changes beyond capitalism and socialism."

"Precisely, Pavan," the Professor confirmed. "There's a growing recognition that traditional economic ideologies haven't fully delivered on their promises of equitable distribution of benefits. Researchers are exploring alternative management styles, and many are looking towards the concept of *Dharma Niti* from Indian scriptures." *This demonstrates the leadership quality of* ***being open to new ideas and exploring alternative approaches***. Leaders should not be confined by traditional thinking and should be willing to look beyond conventional models.

Mythili inquired, "*Dharma Niti*? What does that entail?"

"Dharma Niti, in essence," Professor explained, "is a framework for ethical and righteous conduct, applicable to all aspects of life, including business and management. It emphasizes principles like truthfulness, compassion, integrity, and social responsibility. It's about creating a system where economic activities are not just profitable but also contribute to the well-being of society." *This introduces the leadership principle of* ***ethical and values-based leadership***. Leaders must prioritize ethical conduct and social responsibility alongside profitability.

Pavan asked, "The text also mentions the importance of Sanskrit. Why is that relevant in this context?"

The Professor explained, "Sanskrit is the language in which many of the Indian scriptures containing the principles of Dharma Niti are written. A deep understanding of Sanskrit is considered essential for a thorough grasp of these principles. Interestingly, there's a growing interest in Sanskrit studies in European countries, particularly in institutions like Oxford and Cambridge Universities. They recognize the potential of Dharma-based management models to address the shortcomings of existing systems. "*This illustrates the importance of* ***understanding the cultural and historical context*** *of leadership principles.* Leaders should appreciate the value of tradition and learn from the wisdom of the past.

Mythili observed, "So, it's about drawing wisdom from ancient traditions and applying it to modern challenges."

"Exactly," Professor affirmed. "However, it's important to remember that Dharma Shastra in India has had different interpretations and applications throughout history. There have been streams like Buddhism, Jainism, and Brahmanism, each with its own emphasis." *This underscores the leadership lesson of* ***critical thinking and contextual awareness***. Leaders must be able to discern between different interpretations and apply principles appropriately to specific situations.

Mythili noted, "So, the Guru's Sree Narayana Dharma was a departure from traditional interpretations of Dharma?"

"Indeed," Professor confirmed. "The Guru's focus was on putting humanity into practice, making spirituality relevant to the everyday lives of individuals. *This showcases* ***transformational leadership*** *and the ability to adapt traditional concepts to contemporary needs*. Leaders should be able to inspire and guide changes by making relevant and practical applications of core values."

Professor, taking a sip of hot tea, continued: "The Guru believed that everyone, regardless of their birth, had the right to knowledge, dignity, and opportunity. He saw compassion – *'Arulanpanukamba'* – as the core of true Dharma. He focused that a compassionate person, regardless of their background, could achieve spiritual greatness. *This focuses on **inclusive leadership and the magnitude of compassion***. Leaders should create an environment where everyone feels valued and can reach his full potential."

Pavan asked, "The text mentions the Guru's emphasis on 'Dharma is necessary.' What did he mean by that?"

"The Guru used the phrase "Dharma is necessary" to highlight its supreme importance. He stressed that without Dharma, life is meaningless and actions are without direction. He defined Dharma as the supreme God, the greatest wealth, and the key to success. He even said that Dharma is the cause of the universe in various forms of karma, and that the Supreme Brahman is Dharma itself. He stressed that where there is Dharma, there will be success. He wanted everyone to understand that Dharma helps us develop the consciousness of truth." *This underlines the importance of **purpose-driven leadership and having a strong moral compass***. Leaders should have a clear vision and guide their actions based on profoundly held values. See how Guru has defined Dharma:

> "Dharma alone is the supreme divinity,
> Dharma indeed is the greatest wealth,
> May dharma triumph everywhere
> For the well-being of humanity."

Mythili observed, "It seems like the Guru's concept of Dharma is very comprehensive, encompassing both individual conduct and social responsibility."

"Indeed," Professor confirmed. "He emphasized that Dharma should be applied in all aspects of life, including industrial enterprises. He believed that both workers and employers have a Dharma to follow. He pinpointed the significance of ethical conduct, mutual respect, and cooperation in the workplace. He saw the enterprise as a family, where everyone is a soul sibling. He believed that conflict and division are detrimental to progress, and that resolving disputes amicably is essential for success." *This illustrates the leadership principles of* ***creating a positive work environment and fostering collaboration***. Leaders should promote teamwork, mutual respect, and open communication.

Pavan asked, "So, the Guru's Dharma-based management model is about creating a harmonious and ethical work environment?"

"Precisely," the Professor replied. "It's about fostering unity, mutual trust, and a sense of shared purpose. It's about recognizing the interdependence of workers and employers, and working together for the common goal. It's about creating a system where everyone feels valued, respected, and empowered to contribute to the success of the enterprise and thereby the well-being of society." *This reinforces the importance of* ***employee engagement and empowerment***. Leaders should create a culture where employees feel valued and motivated to contribute their best.

Mythili remarked, "it is a holistic approach that integrates ethical principles, social responsibility, and economic goals."

"Perfectly," Professor concluded. "The Guru's teachings on Dharma provide a valuable framework for creating a more just and sustainable economic system. His vision is as relevant today as it was a century ago, perhaps even more so, as we grapple with the complex challenges of globalization and economic inequality." *This emphasizes the importance of* ***long-term vision and sustainable leadership***. Leaders should consider the broader impact of their decisions and attempt to create a better future for all.

Major Leadership Lessons based on the current discussion were summarized by Mythili as:

- **Anticipating future needs and fostering holistic development:** Recognizing the interconnectedness of different fields and encouraging cross-disciplinary thinking.
- **Being open to new ideas and exploring alternative approaches:** Looking beyond conventional models and adapting to change.
- **Ethical and values-based leadership:** Sequencing ethical conduct and social responsibility.
- **Understanding the cultural and historical context:** Accelerating the value of tradition and learning from the past.
- **Critical thinking and contextual awareness:** Spotting between different interpretations and applying principles appropriately.
- **Transformational leadership:** Inspiring and guiding change by making relevant and practical applications of core values.
- **Inclusive leadership and the importance of compassion:** Creating an environment where everyone feels valued and has the opportunity to reach their full potential.
- **Purpose-driven leadership and having a strong moral compass:** Having a clear vision and guiding actions based on deeply held values.
- **Creating a positive work environment and fostering collaboration:** Promoting teamwork, mutual respect, and open communication.
- **Employee engagement and empowerment:** Creating a culture where employees feel valued and motivated.
- **Long-term vision and sustainable leadership:** Considering the broader impact of decisions and striving to create a better future.

❖ ❖ ❖

8

CREATING OPPORTUNITIES: EMPLOYMENT AND INCOME FOR ALL

Mythili and Pavan reached the Professor's chamber for the discussion of another topic. They sat opposite Professor Siva and the youthful faces were mirroring a mixture of curiosity and anticipation. The air in the Professor's chamber, thick with the scent of old books and brewing coffee, crackled with intellectual energy.

Professor smiled, a hint of pride in his eyes. "Today let us discuss economic empowerment, acknowledging the inherent dignity of labor and the potential for self-reliance. The Guru understood that true liberation could only be achieved through a holistic transformation, one that addressed both the spiritual and material needs of individuals."

Professor rose from his chair and walked towards a bookshelf, his fingers tracing the spines of countless volumes. "The Guru's insights are particularly relevant in our contemporary world, where issues of unemployment, income disparity, and economic stagnation continue to plague societies across the globe. His emphasis on skill development, entrepreneurship, and the promotion of traditional crafts offers valuable lessons even today."

He pulled out a worn leather-bound book and returned to his seat. "Let's begin with the context. Post-independence India, while brimming with acclaimed freedom, faced the daunting task of nation-building. Large-scale industries were being established, but the benefits of this growth often failed to trickle down to the lower strata of the society. Unemployment and lack of purchasing power were rampant. The Guru recognized that the traditional skills and artistry that had been the hallmark of Indian craftsmanship for centuries held the key to economic empowerment."

Mythili interjected, "So, he saw handicrafts not just as a cultural legacy, but as a feasible economic engine?"

"Precisely," Professor affirmed. "He understood the privileges that traditional crafts offered. They needed relatively low capital investment, provided employment opportunities at the grassroots level, particularly for women, and had the potential to generate significant foreign exchange. India's handlooms, handicrafts, coir, and cashew products had a long-standing admiration in the international market. The Guru sought to revitalize these sectors and make them a cornerstone of India's economic resurgence."

Pavan sniggered slightly. "But weren't these traditional industries facing stiff competition from large Corporations, especially with the wave of liberalization, globalization, and privatization?"

"Indeed, they were," the Professor acknowledged. "The market was becoming increasingly dominated by mass-produced goods, threatening the livelihoods of artisans and craftspeople. The Guru was acutely aware of this challenge. He didn't advocate for abandoning large-scale industrialization altogether, but he commended the vital role that the micro and small-scale industries, particularly those centered on handicrafts, could play in balancing the economic landscape."

He opened the book in his hands. "Here, we find a fascinating observation about the unique adroitness of Indian artisans. It's often noted how their hands and fingers, honed through generations of craftsmanship, seem to possess an inherent skill – a dexterity not limited to handicrafts but seen in other fields requiring fine motor skills, like cardiac surgery. The Guru recognized this inherent talent and sought to nurture it."

Mythili leaned forward, her interest piqued . "So, he wasn't just advocating for preserving traditional crafts, but also recognizing the inherent skills and talents of individuals?"

"Absolutely," the Professor replied. "He viewed the potential for excellence in every individual, regardless of his background. He believed that by providing training and opportunities, the talents could be nurtured and transformed into valuable skills. He established weaving units and encouraged the development of coir industries, cashew processing units, and various other handicraft enterprises. He understood that these weren't just about producing goods; they were about empowering individuals, fostering self-reliance, and creating a sense of dignity in labor."

Pavan asked, "Professor, you mentioned that the Guru's teachings transcended community boundaries. How did he ensure that his vision benefited everyone, not just a select few?"

"That's a very important question, Pavan," the Professor said. "The Guru's vision was truly inclusive. He encouraged everyone to embrace the opportunities, regardless of caste or social standing. He comprehended that the skills and talents he sought to cultivate were not confined to any group. He actively promoted education and vocational training for all, believing that knowledge and skills were the keys to social and economic mobility. He understood that true progress could only be achieved when everyone had the opportunity to contribute and benefit."

He paused, taking a sip of his coffee. "The Guru's approach was not just about economic development; it was about social transformation too. He recognized that economic empowerment was inextricably linked to social equality. By providing individuals with the means to earn a respectable livelihood, he helped to break down the fences of caste, social, and economic discrimination. He fostered a sense of community and collaboration, encouraging individuals to work together for the common good"

Mythili observed, "It seems like he was way ahead of his time. His ideas about skill development, entrepreneurship, and inclusive growth are still relevant today."

"Indeed, they are," Professor agreed. "The Guru's teachings offer timeless wisdom. He understood the basic principles of human development and economic empowerment. He recognized the worthiness of nurturing individual talents, promoting self-reliance, and fostering a sense of community. His vision was not just about creating jobs; it was about creating opportunities for individuals to realize their full potential and live a life of dignity."

The Professor closed the book gently. "The Guru's legacy is not just about the specific economic activities he helped to develop; it's about the principles he championed. His emphasis on skill development, entrepreneurship, and inclusive growth is as relevant today as they were a century ago. His teachings offer a strategy for creating a more just and equitable society, where everyone has the chance to thrive."

Pavan pondered for a moment. "Professor, how can we apply these teachings in our own lives? What can we do to contribute to this vision of empowerment and inclusive growth?"

The Professor smiled. "That's the most important question of all, Pavan. The Guru's teachings are not just for governments and policymakers; they are for each one of us. We can start by recognizing the value of all forms of labor, by respecting the skills and talents of others, and by supporting local artisans and craftsmen. We can also stimulate entrepreneurship and innovation by creating opportunities for others to develop their skills and pursue their dreams. And most importantly, we can strive to create a more inclusive society, where everyone has the chance to reach their full potential, regardless of their background or circumstances."

The Professor looked at Mythili and Pavan, his eyes filled with hope. "The Guru's vision is not just a historical legacy; it's a call to action. It's a reminder that each one of us has a role to play in building a better future, a future where we get an opportunity to thrive."

The conversation continued late into the evening, examining various facets of the Guru's teachings and their relevance to the contemporary world. Mythili and Pavan, inspired by the professor's insights, left the chamber with a renewed sense of aspiration. They realized that the Guru's legacy was not just about the past; it was about the future, a future that they could help to shape.

Over the next few weeks, Mythili and Pavan delved deeper into the Guru's life and teachings. They visited local artisan communities, interacted with craftsmen, and learned about the challenges they faced. They also researched successful social enterprises that were applying the Guru's principles of skill development and inclusive growth.

Mythili, with her passion for social justice, decided to focus her research on the impact of the Guru's teachings on women's empowerment. She discovered numerous stories of women who had transformed their lives through vocational training and entrepreneurship. They had gained economic independence, earned the respect of their communities, and become role models for future generations.

Pavan, with his keen interest in economics, explored the potential of sustainable development through traditional crafts. He realized that the Guru's emphasis on local production and consumption was not only economically sound but also environmentally responsible. He saw the potential for creating a circular economy, where resources were used efficiently and waste was minimized.

As they continued their research, Mythili and Pavan realized that the Guru's teachings were not just about specific industries or communities; they were about universal principles that could be applied in any context. They were about recognizing the inherent dignity of labor, fostering self-reliance, and building inclusive communities.

They also discovered that the Guru's influence extended beyond the economic sphere. His emphasis on education and social reforms had laid the foundation for a more progressive and equitable society. His teachings on non-violence and universal brotherhood had inspired generations to fight against social injustice and economic discrimination.

Another afternoon, Mythili and Pavan visited a handloom weaving cooperative society in a nearby village. The rhythmic clatter of looms filled the air, a symphony of human skill and creativity. They spoke with the weavers, mostly women, who shared their stories of struggle and resilience. They learned how the cooperatives had provided them with training, access to markets, and a sense of community. Many of these women had been previously marginalized, struggling to make ends meet. Now, they are skilled artisans, earning a respectable livelihood and supporting their next generation to gain higher education.

Mythili was particularly moved by the story of a young woman named Radha. Radha had been forced to drop out of school at an early age due to financial constraints. She had worked as a domestic helper, earning meager wages and facing constant exploitation. Joining the weaving cooperative had transformed her life. She had learned the intricate art of handloom weaving, developed her own designs, and now sold her creations at local markets and even online taking the services of the co-operatives. She was no longer just a wage earner; she was an entrepreneur, a creator, a woman with a newfound sense of confidence and self-worth.

"The Guru's vision is alive and well here," Mythili whispered to Pavan, her eyes filled with admiration. "These women are living proof of the transformative power of his teachings."

Pavan nodded in agreement. "It's not just about the economic benefits," he observed. "It's about the dignity, the sense of purpose, the empowerment that these women have gained. It's about the ripple effect it has on their families and their community."

As they left the cooperative, Mythili and Pavan discussed how they could contribute to this movement. They decided to use their skills and knowledge to promote these traditional crafts and support the artisans. Mythili, with her passion for writing and communication, planned to create a blog and social media campaign to showcase the beauty and value of handloom products. Pavan, with his understanding of business and marketing, explored ways to connect artisans directly with consumers, cutting out intermediaries and ensuring fairer prices.

They also realized the importance of education and awareness. They decided to organize workshops and seminars in schools and colleges to educate young people about the rich heritage of Indian handicrafts and the potential for careers in this sector. They wanted to motivate the next generation to appreciate and support these traditional skills, ensuring their survival in the face of rapid technological advancements.

After a few days, they visited Professor Siva to share their experiences and ideas. The Professor listened attentively, his face beaming with pride.

"I'm so heartened to see your excitement and commitment," he said. "You have truly grasped the essence of the Guru's teachings. He did not just want to create jobs; he wanted to create a movement, a crusade of empowerment, self-reliance, and social transformation. And you are now part of that campaign."

He shared stories of other individuals and organizations that were working to promote traditional crafts and empower artisans. The Guru spoke of designers who were incorporating handloom fabrics into contemporary fashion, creating a new market for those products. He mentioned social entrepreneurs who were using technology to connect artisans with global markets, providing them with access to wider markets and better prices.

"The possibilities are endless," Professor Siva said. "The Guru's vision is a seed that has been planted, and it continues to grow and flourish. It's up to us to nurture that seed, to cultivate it, and to ensure that it continues to bear fruit for generations to come."

He paused, his gaze sweeping across their faces. "But the journey is far from over. The challenges facing traditional crafts and artisan communities are complex and multifaceted. Globalization, technological advancements, and changing consumer preferences continue to disrupt the economic landscape. We must remain vigilant, adapting our strategies and seeking new ways to support these vital sectors."

Mythili nodded in agreement. "We've realized that it's not just about preserving traditions; it's about innovation and adaptation. We need to find ways to integrate traditional skills with modern technologies, creating products that are both beautiful and relevant to contemporary lifestyles."

Pavan added, "We also need to address the issue of market access. Many artisans struggle to reach consumers directly, often relying on intermediaries who take a significant cut of their profits. We need to explore new models of distribution and marketing, leveraging technology to connect artisans with global markets and ensure fair prices."

Professor encouraged their proactive thinking. "Indeed, innovation and adaptability are vital. The Guru himself was a champion of progress, embracing new ideas and technologies while remaining rooted in the values of tradition and community. He understood that progress was not about abandoning the past, but about building upon it, creating a future that was both modern and sustainable."

The Professor leaned forward, his eyes sparkling with wisdom. "And remember, the most important aspect of this work is not just the economic benefits, but the social and cultural impact. By supporting traditional crafts, we are not just preserving skills and livelihoods; we are conserving a way of life, a sense of community, and a connection to our heritage."

He spoke of the importance of cultural tourism, creating opportunities for travelers to experience the rich traditions and craftsmanship of local communities. He emphasized the role of education, raising awareness among young people about the value of traditional skills and the potential for careers in this sector.

"We need to create a society where artisans are not just seen as producers of goods, but as custodians of culture, as storytellers, as keepers of traditions," he said. "Their skills are not just economic assets; they are cultural treasures that must be cherished and conserved."

Mythili and Pavan were deeply moved by the Professor's words. They realized that their work was not just about promoting handicrafts; it was about promoting a way of life, a philosophy of empowerment, self-reliance, and community. It was about creating a society where everyone had the opportunity to thrive, where skills and talents were valued, and where the dignity of labor was admired.

They left the Professor's chamber with a renewed sense of mission, their hearts filled with gratitude and determination. They knew that the journey ahead would be challenging, but they were confident that, with the guidance of the Guru's teachings and the support of the community, they could continue to weave the threads of change, creating a more just, equitable, and sustainable world for all.

Pavan summarized the current session as:

1. **Traditional Crafts as an Economic Engine:** The Guru appreciated the potential of traditional crafts (handlooms, coir, handicrafts, etc.) not just as cultural artifacts, but as viable economic drivers, particularly in post-independence India. They require low capital investment, offer grassroots employment (especially for women), and can generate foreign exchange.
2. **Balancing Large-Scale Industry with Micro, Small, and Medium Enterprises:** The Guru understood the need for both large-scale industrialization and the support of micro, small and medium industries, especially those focused on the handicrafts, so as to create a balanced economic landscape.
3. **Skill Development as a Foundation for Empowerment:** The Guru emphasized the importance of nurturing inherent talents and providing training to transform the talents into valuable skills, leading to economic self-reliance and dignity of labor.
4. **Inclusive Growth and Breaking down Barriers:** The Guru's vision was inclusive, encouraging everyone, regardless of caste or social standing, to embrace economic opportunities. He promoted education and vocational training for all, recognizing knowledge and skills as keys to social and economic mobility.

5. **Entrepreneurship and Self-Reliance:** The Guru fostered entrepreneurship by establishing handloom weaving units, coir industries, cashew processing units, and other handicraft enterprises, promoting self-reliance and empowering individuals.
6. **Connecting Artisans with Markets:** The narrative highlights the ongoing need to connect artisans directly with consumers, cutting out intermediaries to ensure fairer prices and broader market access, potentially through technology.
7. **Innovation and Adaptation:** The story emphasizes the importance of innovation and adapting traditional skills to modern technologies and consumer preferences to ensure the continued relevance and sustainability of traditional crafts. It's not just about preserving the past, but building upon it.
8. **The Importance of Cultural Tourism and Education:** The narrative suggests leveraging cultural tourism to showcase traditional crafts and raise awareness among young people about the value and potential of careers in the sector.
9. **Beyond Economic Benefits:** The story underscores that the value of supporting traditional crafts goes beyond the economic gains. They include preserving cultural heritage, fostering a sense of community, promoting social equality, and recognizing the dignity of all forms of labor.

❖ ❖ ❖

9

Nourishing the Nation: Strengthening Agriculture

The monsoon rain drummed a steady rhythm against the windows of Professor's chamber, its cadence blending with the soft crackle of the fireplace. The room was steeped in warmth and wisdom, a sanctuary of thought amid the storm outside.

"Today, my dear students," Professor Siva began, his voice resonant with the weight of years spent pondering great ideas, "we delve into the heart of the Guru's vision for agriculture — a sector he held as the lifeblood of a nation, particularly one like India, striving to rise from the shadows of economic disparity."

Mythili, her gaze drifting to the rain-streaked window pane, where rivulets traced fleeting patterns, mused aloud, "Professor, why did the Guru, a champion of social reform, place such emphasis on agriculture? Was it merely to ensure economic sustenance for a fledgling nation?"

Professor's eyes twinkled in the firelight, reflecting both amusement and pride. "Ah, Mythili, the Guru's wisdom was a river with many currents. He saw agriculture not as a mere economic retainer but as the soul of India — a force capable of sustaining life, facilitating equity, and preserving the cultural identity. He believed that a nation's strength lies in its ability to feed itself, to empower its people, and to grow from the soil upward."

He reached for a weathered copy of the Guru's writings resting on the table, its edges softened by time, its pages marked with underlines and annotations in faded ink. "In a land where nearly fifty percent of the people depend on agriculture and allied areas for their livelihoods," he read aloud, "The Guru argued that its revitalization was the key to unlocking economic prosperity and social justice. He saw it as the bedrock of self-reliance, a shield against foreign dependency."

Pavan, ever the pragmatist, leaned forward, his brow furrowed. "But Professor, how do we reconcile the Guru's lofty ideals with the ground realities of Indian agriculture? Small landholdings averaging less than two hectares, fragmented markets riddled with middlemen, and farmers trapped in a debt cycle — some owing as much as fifty thousand rupees to local moneylenders at exorbitant rates of twenty to thirty percent interest per annum. These are not small hurdles."

Professor nodded gravely, his fingers tracing the spine of the book. "The Guru was no dreamer detached from reality, Pavan. He knew the farmer's plight intimately — how a single failed monsoon could plunge a family into ruin, how the lack of capital forced them to sell their produce at distress prices, often as low as ten rupees per quintal for rice when middlemen later sold it for triple that amount. His vision was a practical one, rooted in both modern innovation and timeless wisdom."

Professor opened the book to a dog-eared page and read, " The farmer must not be a mere tiller of soil, but a master of his destiny.' The Guru proposed a multi-pronged approach: integrating scientific farming techniques — such as crop rotation and soil testing — to boost yields, while preserving traditional practices like mixed cropping that sustained the land. But he didn't stop there. He saw financial empowerment as the linchpin."

Mythili tilted her head, intrigued. "Financial empowerment? Did he mean loans and subsidies?"

"More than that," the Professor replied, setting the book down. "The Guru visualized a financial ecosystem tailored to the farmer's needs. He urged the creation of rural cooperative banks and credit societies — imagine a network where a farmer could borrow at a modest four percent interest instead of the crippling rates charged by the indigenous moneylenders. He envisioned that if a farmer with a two-hectare plot borrowed ten thousand rupees to buy quality seeds and fertilizers, a good harvest could yield a surplus of fifteen to twenty thousand rupees after repaying the loan, breaking the debt cycle."

Pavan scribbled a quick note in his notebook, his mind racing. "So, he wanted to replace exploitative moneylenders with a system that worked for the farmers. But how would these cooperatives fund themselves?"

"Through collective strength," the Professor explained. "The Guru proposed that farmers' pool small contributions — say, fifty rupees each from a hundred members — to create a corpus. This fund, managed transparently, could offer loans and even insure against crop failure. He drew inspiration from European cooperatives, like those in Denmark, where farmers collectively owned dairies and earned steady profits — sometimes doubling their income within a decade. In India, he saw this model scaling to millions, with government support to kickstart it." The Guru sought insights from various sources, including his diverse disciples, on these matters.

Mythili's eyes widened with realization. "So, the Guru saw farmers not just as producers, but as entrepreneurs — '*agripreneurs*,' as you called it?"

"Exactly!" The professor's voice rose with enthusiasm. "He believed every farmer could diversify his income. Take a smallholder with two hectares: alongside paddy, he could cultivate high-value crops like turmeric or saffron, which fetch prices of two hundred rupees per kilogram or more. Add a few dairy cows — yielding ten liters of milk daily at thirty rupees per liter — and suddenly, his monthly income jumps from a precarious two thousand rupees to over fifteen thousand. The Guru even suggested agro-processing — turning raw paddy into rice and rice powder or rubber into rubber-based products — adding another twenty to thirty percent to his earnings."

Pavan tapped his pen against his chin. "But what about market access? Even with higher yields or processed goods, farmers still get squeezed by middlemen. I read that in all States in India, they pocket sixty percent of the final sales proceeds."

Professor leaned back; his expression resolute. "The Guru foresaw this chokehold. He proposed farmer-owned marketing cooperatives to cut out the intermediaries. Picture this: a cooperative collects produce from fifty farmers — say, a hundred quintals of paddy — negotiates directly with urban buyers or exports it, securing thirty rupees per quintal instead of ten. That is an extra two thousand rupees per farmer per harvest. He also pushed for rural infrastructure — warehouses to store grain, preventing distress sales, and roads to connect villages to markets, reducing transport costs from five rupees per kilometer to two."

He paused, then added, "And value addition was the key. A farmer selling raw rubber might earn fifty rupees per unit, but if he spins it into sheets, that jumps to eighty. The Guru calculated that if just ten percent of

India's farmers adopted such practices for their rural income could rise by billions of rupees annually."

Mythili sipped her tea, her mind alight with possibilities. "And sustainability — how did he tie that to finances?"

"The Guru was ahead of his time," Professor said, his tone reverent. "He championed organic farming not just for the land's sake, but for profit. Chemical fertilizers cost a farmer five hundred rupees per hectare each season, often with diminishing returns. Indigenous seeds and compost, though labor-intensive, cost a fraction — assume fifty rupees — and maintain soil fertility. He cited examples from Santiniketan, where organic plots outlasted chemically farmed ones by decades, saving farmers thousands in the long run. Plus, organic produce fetches a premium — sometimes fifty percent more in the cities.

Pavan frowned thoughtfully. "But scaling this — training millions of farmers, building cooperatives, funding banks — it would need massive investment. Where would the money come from?"

The Professor smiled knowingly. "The Guru had an answer for that, too. He proposed an agricultural fund, seeded with a modest tax — say, one percent — on urban industries, which rely on rural raw materials anyway. He estimated that in the 1920s India, this could raise fifty crore rupees annually. Reinvested into cooperatives, schools, and research, it would grow exponentially. He also called on wealthy zamindars to contribute, not as charity, but as stakeholders in a thriving rural economy that would stabilize their own incomes."

Mythili set her cup down, her voice firm with conviction. "So, the Guru's vision wasn't just about feeding India — it was about creating a just society, where farmers weren't pawns but partners in progress, where each rupee they earned strengthened the nation."

"Precisely," Professor affirmed. "He saw agriculture as India's economic engine — capable of generating crores in wealth, employing millions, and slashing poverty. A farmer earning five thousand rupees a month instead of five hundred could send his children to school, buy home utensils, and build a pucca house. Rural prosperity would slow migration to cities, easing urban strain, and preserve our agrarian heritage — our songs, our festivals, our bond with the earth."

As the rain outside softened to a gentle drizzle, Mythili and Pavan stepped out of the chamber, their minds buzzing with the Guru's vision. The financial details — cooperative loans at five percent, organic savings of hundreds per hectare, market profits doubled through collective bargaining — intertwined a tapestry of possibility. They carried not just his ideals but a blueprint: a future where agriculture wasn't a burden but a boon, where the land's bounty lifted every hand that tilled it. In nurturing that vision, they knew they were nurturing the soul of India itself.

Mythili summarized the discussion in the session as:

- **Agriculture as the Soul of India:** The Guru saw agriculture not just as an economic activity, but as the foundation of India's identity, prosperity, and self-reliance.
- **Financial Empowerment of Farmers:** He emphasized the need to break the cycle of debt by providing farmers access to affordable credit through cooperative banks and credit societies.
- **Cooperatives for Collective Strength:** The Guru advocated for farmer-owned cooperatives to pool resources, share knowledge, and negotiate better prices for their produce. .
- **Agripreneurship:** The guru encouraged farmers to become entrepreneurs, diversifying their income through high-value crops, animal husbandry, and agro-processing.

- **Market Access and Value Addition:** The Guru envisioned farmer-owned marketing boards to bypass middlemen and ensure fair prices. He also emphasized value addition to increase income.
- **Sustainable Agriculture:** The Guru promoted organic farming and sustainable practices, recognizing their long-term economic and environmental benefits.
- **Investment in Rural Infrastructure:** The Guru called for investments in rural infrastructure, such as warehouses and roads, to reduce costs and improve market access.
- **National Agricultural Fund:** The Guru proposed an agricultural fund to support agricultural development, funded by a tax on urban industries and contributions from wealthy landowners.
- **Agriculture as an Engine of Growth:** The Guru believed that a thriving agricultural sector could drive economic growth, reduce poverty, and create a more equitable and sustainable society.

❖ ❖ ❖

10

The Sivagiri Model: A Vision for Agro-Industrial Development

The monsoon rain painted streaks of silver across the windows of Professor's Chamber, the rhythmic dialogue a soothing backdrop to the animated conversation within. The scent of sandalwood incense mingled with the aroma of freshly brewed coffee, creating an atmosphere of warmth and intellectual curiosity. Professor Siva, his face etched with the wisdom of a sage, held a slim volume bound in faded blue cloth, its edges worn from years of reverent handling.

"Today, my dear students," he began, his voice echoing with a quiet intensity, "we explore a fascinating lesson in the legacy of the Guru – the Sivagiri Agro-Industrial Gurukula Project, a visionary plan conceived by his devoted disciple, Swami Ernest Kirk."

Mythili, her eyes wide with surprise, exclaimed, "Swami Ernest Kirk? I've never heard of him, Professor! Was he an Indian disciple?"

"Ah, Mythili," Professor chuckled warmly, "Swami Kirk was no ordinary disciple. He was an Englishman, a seeker of truth who traversed the vast spiritual landscape of India, eventually finding inspiration and enlightenment in the teachings of the Guru."

The Professor opened the book, revealing a faded photograph of a man with kind eyes and a flowing beard, dressed in simple saffron robes. "Ernest Kirk was a Theosophist who arrived in India in the early 20th century, attracted by the wisdom of the East. He met the Guru at the behest of Ramana Maharshi, who saw in Kirk a kindred spirit – a man who could bridge the philosophies of East and West with practical accomplishments."

Pavan, his curiosity piqued, leaned forward. "Professor, what was so special about this Swami Kirk? Why did the Guru entrust him with such an ambitious project?"

"Swami Kirk possessed a rare blend of spiritual insight and practical acumen," the Professor explained. "He wasn't just a dreamer; he was a doer. He understood the Guru's vision for a society built on education, self-reliance, and economic empowerment. He saw agriculture and industry not as mere vocation, but as engines of expansion that could lift entire communities out of poverty."

Professor leaned back in his chair; his gaze distant as if recalling a memory. "Let me tell you a story about Swami Kirk that a few know. In 1924, during a drought in Travancore, Swami Kirk visited a small village called *Kalluvayal*. The farmers there were on the brink of despair – their crops had withered, and moneylenders circled like vultures. Kirk didn't just offer prayers; he brought with him a hand-drawn blueprint for a low-cost irrigation system, using bamboo pipes and a simple gravity-fed reservoir. Within weeks, the villagers had water flowing to their fields again, and the harvest that followed paid off their debts."

Mythili's jaw dropped. "He built a low-cost irrigation system? That is incredible!"

"Indeed," the Professor said with a nod. "That's the kind of man he was – a spiritual seeker with a farmer's stamina. The Guru saw this and knew Kirk could turn the Sivagiri vision into reality."

He continued, "The Guru believed that true progress wasn't just about spiritual awakening; it required material well-being too. Agriculture was India's lifeblood, employing millions. But it was shackled by outdated methods and exploitation.

The Gurukula Project aimed to change that by integrating modern agricultural science with traditional wisdom and creating a model that was both financially viable and socially transformative."

Mythili, her brow wrinkled in thought, interjected, "But Professor, wasn't the Guru more focused on social reform – eradicating caste discrimination and uplifting the downtrodden? How did agriculture fit into that?"

Professor Siva smiled patiently. "Social reform and economic empowerment were two sides of the same coin for the Guru, Mythili. He knew that caste and poverty were intertwined. By giving people the tools to earn a living – through farming, crafts, or small industries – they could break those chains. The Gurukula wasn't just a school; it was a revolution disguised as education."

He gestured toward the book, flipping to a yellowed page filled with meticulous diagrams. "*The Sivagiri Agro-Industrial Gurukula* Project was designed as a self-sustaining rural university in the long run. It would teach students modern farming techniques – crop rotation, organic fertilizers, water management – alongside skills like weaving, pottery, and metalwork. But here's the genius: it was not just about learning. The

Gurukula would produce goods – rice, cotton, tools – and sell them in local markets, reinvesting the profits to expand the project."

Pavan, ever the pragmatist, raised an eyebrow. "Professor, that sounds impressive, but was it economically feasible? How would it compete with big landlords or urban industries?"

"Good question, Pavan," the Professor said, his eyes gleaming with enthusiasm. "Swami Kirk had thought this through. He studied the local economy and saw that small farmers were crushed by the middlemen who bought their produces cheap and sold it dear. The Gurukula would cut out those parasites by creating cooperatives – farmers pooling their resources, sharing equipment, and selling directly to buyers. Kirk even calculated that with just 50 acres of well-managed land, the Gurukula could generate enough surplus to fund scholarships for a hundred students within three years."

To illustrate, the Professor recounted another tale. "In 1931, Swami Kirk ran a small experiment near Sivagiri Hill. He convinced ten families to grow a new strain of drought-resistant millet he'd sourced from a Botanist friend in Madras. They used compost from cattle waste – free and abundant – instead of expensive fertilizers. That year, while other fields failed, their harvest doubled. They sold the surplus in Kochi, earning enough to buy a shared bullock cart. That cart became their lifeline, carrying goods to market and cutting transport costs. Kirk proved that with the right knowledge and cooperation; rural India could thrive."

Mythili clapped her hands, inspired. "That's brilliant! It is like a business plan rooted in compassion!"

"Exactly," the Professor said. "The Gurukula's financial viability was attributed to come from its simplicity. It was not intended to rely on charity or government handouts. It would leverage what was already there – land, labor, and local ingenuity – and turn it into wealth. Kirk even proposed a small bank within the Gurukula, offering microloans to farmers at fair rates, breaking the grip of predatory lenders."

Pavan scratched his chin. "So, Professor, was this project just an idealistic dream, or did it actually happen?"

The Professor's expression softened, tinged with melancholy. "Sadly, Pavan, it never fully took root. Swami Kirk poured his heart into it – planned to travel across Kerala, for raising funds, sketching plans – but the odds were stacked against him. And after the Guru's passing in 1928, internal squabbles among his followers stalled the momentum."

He paused, then shared a poignant memory. "I once met an old man in Sivagiri who remembered Kirk. He was a boy then, watching Kirk teach villagers to build a loom from scrap wood. 'That loom fed my family for years,' the man told me, his eyes misty. 'But when the Guru left, the dream faded.' Kirk opted out of Sivagiri Mutt in 1939, broken by exhaustion, and the Gurukula remained a blueprint."

Mythili's voice rose with determination. "Professor, we can't let it stay a blueprint! India still needs this – rural unemployment, climate change, the urban-rural divide – the Gurukula as envisaged by Swami Kirk could solve so much!"

Pavan nodded, warming to the idea. "She's right. With today's tech – solar power, e-commerce, biotech crops – we could make it even more profitable. Imagine a Gurukula selling organic turmeric online, or exporting handicrafts to Europe or other parts of the world."

Professor's eyes twinkled with hope. "You're both onto something. Picture this: a modern Gurukula with a startup mindset. Students learn hydroponics, earning income from urban rooftop farms. Artisans use 3D printers to craft designs rooted in tradition, tapping global markets.

A cooperative app connects farmers to buyers, ensuring fair prices. The revenue funds more schools, spreading the model nationwide."

Professor leaned forward; his voice alive with possibility. "Financially, it's sound. A pilot project on 20 acres could break even in two years, with profits scaling as students graduate and start their own ventures. Economically, it is a multiplier – every rupee invested in rural skills creates three more in the community. And socially, it's a lifeline for millions."

Mythili grinned. "Professor, let's do it! We will pitch it to investors, Non-Governmental Organisations (NGOs), the government – anyone who will listen!"

Pavan added, "I'll crunch the numbers. We'll make it irresistible – a legacy reborn with hard data to back it up."

As the rain subsided and the evening sky glowed with the promise of a new dawn, Mythili and Pavan left the Professor's Chamber, their hearts ablaze with purpose. They carried with them the legacy of Swami Ernest Kirk – the Englishman who saw India's soul – and the enduring wisdom of the Guru. It was a call to action, a chance to weave tradition and modernity into a tapestry of progress, to plant seeds of change in the fertile soil of their motherland, and to prove that a dream deferred could still bloom into a revolution.

Key Learnings of the customer session, scribbled by Pavan:

- **Swami Ernest Kirk, the Bridge Builder:** An English Theosophist who became a devoted disciple of the Guru, embodying a blend of spiritual insight and practical action.
- **Guru's Vision of Holistic Progress:** True progress encompasses both spiritual awakening and material well-being, with agriculture and industry as key drivers.

- **Sivagiri Agro-Industrial Gurukula Project:** A visionary plan for a self-sustaining rural university, combining education, skills training, and economic empowerment, drafted by Swami Kirk as directed by the Guru.
- **Economic Empowerment through Education and Skills:** The Gurukula aimed to teach modern agricultural and industrial techniques alongside traditional crafts, creating a skilled workforce and entrepreneurs.
- **Financial Viability through Cooperatives and Direct Marketing:** The project emphasized cooperatives to eliminate middlemen, ensuring fair prices for the farmers and artisans.
- **Innovation and Sustainability:** The Gurukula was planned as a hub for innovation, exploring new techniques and technologies, while promoting sustainable practices.
- **Microfinance and Access to Capital:** The project included a microfinance component, offering loans at fair rates to break the grip of predatory lenders.
- **A Dream Deferred, But Not Forgotten:** Despite Swami Kirk's efforts, the project never fully materialized due to internal conflicts.
- **Relevance for Today's Challenges:** The Gurukula's vision remains relevant for addressing issues like unemployment, climate change, and the urban-rural divide.

❖ ❖ ❖

11

Business at the Core: Exploring Economic Themes at Sivagiri

In the quiet, book-lined study of Professor, a worn pamphlet held center stage. The scent of old paper and incense filled the air as Mythili and Pavan waited, their attention drawn to the Professor's every move. Outside, rain provided a gentle, rhythmic backdrop.

"Today," he began, his voice a low, resonant hum that filled the quiet room, "we dig into this Guru's vision for trade, a subject he deemed crucial for the prosperity of the nation. A vision often overlooked, but no less vital." He paused, allowing the weight of his words to settle. "Imagine," he said, "a sunlit village nestled amidst the rolling hills of Kerala, a gentle breeze carrying the scent of spices and the hum of industrious hands at work. To him, trade was not merely the exchange of goods; it was the lifeblood of a thriving society."

Pavan, his brow furrowed in concentration, leaned forward, his gaze intense. "Professor, I understand the Guru's emphasis on education and industry, his push for self-reliance. But why trade? Why was it so important to him? It seems...secondary."

"Ah, Pavan," the Professor smiled, a warm, knowing smile that crinkled the corners of his eyes. "The Guru understood that production without distribution was like a river without an outlet, a magnificent source rendered useless without a channel. He saw trade as the vital link between the producer and the consumer, a conduit for economic growth and social well-being. A bridge, if you will, connecting the seeds of labor to the fruits of wellness."

He gestured towards the pamphlet, tapping it gently with his finger. "The Guru included 'trade' as one of the eight topics for discussion at the Sivagiri pilgrimage conferences, a series of gatherings meant to ignite a national awakening. This wasn't merely a suggestion; it was a call to action, a strategic imperative. He recognized that trade, when conducted ethically and efficiently, could empower individuals, generate wealth, and foster national self-reliance, building a foundation for a truly independent nation." He quoted the Guru, "What is a harvest if it rots in the fields? What is a woven cloth if it never warms a soul?"

Mythili, her interest piqued, her dark eyes sparkling with curiosity, inquired, "But Professor, what was trade like in the Guru's time? Was it very different from what we see today? The world was so much smaller then, wasn't it?"

"Indeed, Mythili," the Professor replied, his voice taking on a historical tone. "In the Guru's era, in India, trade was largely confined to traditional markets and barter systems, limited by geographical constraints and social barriers. The concept of organized commerce, with its sophisticated distribution networks and marketing strategies, was still in its budding stages, a glimmer on the horizon. The Guru, with his far-reaching vision, foresaw the transformative potential of modern trade, recognizing its ability to bridge geographical distances, connect producers with consumers across vast landscapes, and stimulate economic activity on an unprecedented scale."

He carefully opened the pamphlet, revealing a list of recommendations for promoting trade, the script meticulously penned in elegant calligraphy. "The Guru advocated for the establishment of trade associations, platforms for collective bargaining, and knowledge sharing. He stressed the dissemination of market information, empowering producers with the knowledge they needed to thrive. And he emphasized the development of efficient transportation systems, recognizing that goods needed to move swiftly and reliably. He also stressed the importance of quality control and ethical business practices, ensuring that trade benefited both the producer and the consumer, nurturing a culture of trust and fairness." He added, 'Profit built on deceit is a house built on sand — it will crumble,' the Guru taught.

Pavan, ever the pragmatist, raised a question, his voice laced with concern. "Professor, how did the Guru propose to address the issue of middlemen, those intermediaries who often exploited both the producer and the consumer, sucking the fruits of their efforts?"

"The Guru believed in empowering producers to take control of their own destinies," Professor explained, his voice filled with conviction. "He encouraged the formation of co-operatives, where producers could collectively market their goods, negotiate fair prices, and bypass exploitative intermediaries. He also advocated for the establishment of direct marketing channels, connecting producers directly with consumers through exhibitions, fairs, and retail outlets, cutting out the middleman and ensuring fair returns." He quoted, "cut out the exploiter, and let the wings of your labor lift you."

He shared a story from the Guru's time, his voice softening with nostalgia. "There was a small village, nestled amidst rolling hills, known for the home-based handloom weaving, each piece a masterpiece of intricate craftsmanship. The weavers were struggling to make both ends meet, their livelihoods threatened by unscrupulous middlemen who forced them to sell their products at lower prices. Inspired by the Guru's teachings, they formed a cooperative, pooled their resources, and established a retail outlet in nearby places, a beacon of hope in a sea of despair. They were able to market the cotton products directly to consumers at reasonable prices, significantly increasing their income and improving their livelihoods, regenerating dignity to their craft."

Mythili, her eyes shining with understanding and a newfound appreciation, exclaimed, "So, the Guru saw trade not just as a means of generating profit, but also as a tool for social empowerment, a lever for uplifting communities?"

"Precisely, Mythili," Professor affirmed, his eyes gleaming with pride. "The Guru recognized that trade, when conducted ethically and efficiently, could create opportunities for individuals from all walks of life, regardless of their caste or social standing, breaking down the rigid barriers of conventions and superstitions. He saw it as a means of breaking down social barriers, promoting economic equality, and furthering a sense of community, building a society where everyone had the chance to prosper." He reminded them, "let trade be the river that washes away inequality."

Professor continued, "the Guru's vision for trade extended beyond the domestic market, reaching across oceans and continents. He recognized the importance of international trade, advocating for the export of Indian goods to global markets, showcasing the nation's rich heritage and abundant resources. He believed that India had a rich heritage of craftsmanship, a legacy passed down through generations, and a wealth of natural resources, a treasure trove waiting to be discovered, that could be showcased to the world, generating foreign exchange and boosting the national economy, solidifying India's place on the global stage." He quoted the Guru, "Our spices perfume the air, our silks dazzle the eye - why should they not grace the tables and shoulders of the world?"

Pavan, his mind racing with possibilities, the gears turning with newfound inspiration, asked, "Professor, how can we apply the Guru's teachings to the modern context of e-commerce and knowledge economy, a world vastly different from the Guru's time?"

"The Guru's principles are timeless, Pavan," the Professor replied, his voice filled with steady conviction. "His emphasis on ethical business practices, fair trade, and consumer empowerment remains as relevant today as it was a century ago, perhaps even more so. We can leverage the power of e-commerce, the digital marketplace that transcends geographical boundaries, to connect producers directly with consumers, bypassing intermediaries and ensuring fair prices, creating a level playing field for all. We can also promote sustainable trade practices, ensuring that our economic activities do not harm the environment or exploit vulnerable communities, safeguarding the future for generations to come." He added, "Remember, the Guru taught us, 'a consumer who knows, is a consumer who thrives.' We must awaken the consumer. "The handmade products of Kerala are well-liked in the International market".

The Professor shared a modern example, his eyes lighting up with enthusiasm. "Think of a group of artisans in a remote village, nestled in the foothills of the Himalayas, producing exquisite handicrafts, each piece a testament to their skill and artistry. Through an online platform, a digital storefront accessible to the world, they can showcase their products to a global audience, reaching customers in distant lands, from the bustling streets of Tokyo to the serene shores of California. They can receive fair prices for their work, bypassing middlemen and improving their livelihoods, empowering themselves and their community. This is the power of e-commerce, enabling micro and small producers to participate in the global economy, to share their talents with the world."

Mythili, her voice filled with conviction, her spirit ignited by the Guru's vision, declared, "Professor, we must revive the Guru's vision for trade!

We must promote ethical business practices, support small producers, and ensure that trade benefits all members of society, not just a privileged few. We must strengthen the cooperatives!"

"Indeed, Mythili," Professor agreed, his voice resonating with a sense of purpose. "The Guru's teachings on trade provide a roadmap for building a more just and equitable society, a society where prosperity is shared by all. By promoting ethical business practices, empowering producers with the tools and knowledge they need to thrive, and fostering consumer awareness, we can create a trading system that benefits all, contributing to the prosperity of our nation and the well-being of the people, building a future where everyone has the opportunity to flourish." He reminded them of the Guru's words, "Together, you are a mountain; apart, you are but pebbles."

He paused, a thoughtful expression on his face. "The Guru even placed trade alongside spiritual and social topics at the Sivagiri pilgrimage. 'To study trade,' he explained, 'is to study life itself.' He saw it as a discipline worthy of reflection, a subject that shaped destinies and deserved reverence. Pilgrims who once sought only enlightenment of the soul left with a new understanding — that the marketplace, too, was a domain of purpose and possibility."

"And remember," Professor continued, "the Guru understood that a strong production system was incomplete without an equally sturdy distribution network. He said, 'Production is the seed, but distribution is the rain — neither thrives without the other.' He envisioned trade as the arteries of an economy, ensuring that every product found its purpose, every labor its reward."

As the rain outside subsided, the clouds parting to reveal a sliver of the evening sky, Mythili and Pavan left the study, their minds buzzing with new ideas and a renewed appreciation for the Guru's vision for trade. They carried with them the seeds of his teachings, ready to plant them in the fertile soil of their own endeavors, to cultivate a future where trade served as a force for good, a catalyst for positive change. The lingering scent of sandalwood and old paper served as a gentle reminder of the wisdom they had received, a beacon guiding them on their path. They understood that the Guru's story was not just one of trade, but of humanity — of a man who saw in every sack of rice, every bolt of cloth, a chance to build a better world. Under that banyan tree, he planted seeds of fairness, empowerment, and connection, and today, they bloom in markets near and far, a testament to a sage who traded in hope.

He paused, a thoughtful expression on his face. "The Guru even placed trade alongside spiritual and social topics at the Sivagiri pilgrimage. 'To study trade,' he explained, 'is to study life itself.' He saw it as a discipline worthy of reflection, a subject that shaped destinies and deserved reverence. Pilgrims who once sought only enlightenment of the soul left with a new understanding — that the marketplace, too, was a realm of purpose and possibility."

"And remember," Professor continued, "the Guru understood that a strong production system was incomplete without an equally robust distribution network. He said, 'Production is the seed, but distribution is the rain — neither thrives without the other.' He envisioned trade as the arteries of an economy, ensuring that every good found its purpose, every labor its reward."

Professor Siva provided Mythili and Pavan with the summary of the discussion on trade:

- **Trade as a Vital Link:** The Guru visualized trade as a crucial connection between producers and consumers, driving economic growth.
- **Ethical Trade Practices:** The Guru emphasized fair dealings, quality control, and ethical business conduct.

- **Empowerment of Producers:** The Guru advocated for cooperatives and direct marketing channels to bypass middlemen and ensure fair prices.
- **Social Empowerment through Trade:** Trade was viewed as a tool to break down social barriers and promote economic equality.
- **International Trade:** The Guru appreciated the importance of exporting Indian goods to global markets.
- **Modern Relevance:** The guru's principles remain relevant in the age of e-commerce, globalization, and the knowledge economy.
- **Consumer Awareness:** The Guru stressed the importance of informing consumers about product quality and pricing.
- **Cooperative Models:** The Guru observed the cooperative structures as a way to bolster small producers.
- **Trade as a Subject of Study:** By including trade as a topic for the Sivagiri pilgrimage, the Guru highlighted the need for refreshing and updating the knowledge to cope with the changes in the consumer choices.
- **Distribution is as important as production:** The Guru advised that a strong production system needs a strong distribution system to thrive.

❖ ❖ ❖

12

The Digital Age: From Barter to Bytes

Professor Siva adjusted the projector, the ancient map of Kerala morphing into a timeline depicting the evolution of trade. "Today," he began, his voice imbued with the weight of history, "we trace the arc of commerce, from its rudimentary beginnings to the digital age. We'll examine the financial learnings embedded within each stage, and how they shaped Kerala's economic landscape."

He pointed to the earliest segment of the timeline. "Our journey begins with the Barter. In the pre-monetary era, exchange was direct. A fisherman traded his catch for a farmer's rice. This was the foundation of economic interaction. Mythili, what were the inherent limitations of this system?"

Mythili, her gaze fixed on the timeline, responded, "The 'double coincidence of wants' was a major hurdle. Both parties had to desire what the other possessed. Also, it was difficult to determine the relative value of various goods. A basket of fish might not be equal to a basket of rice, leading to disputes."

"Precisely," Professor agreed. "These limitations spurred the transition to the Trader stage. The emergence of specialized merchants who acted as intermediaries. They traveled, accumulated goods, and facilitated exchange. Pavan, what financial skills were essential for these early traders?"

Pavan, his mind picturing the bustling marketplaces of old, answered, "They needed to be skilled negotiators, risk assessors, and accountants, even if they didn't call it in that way. They had to manage inventory, calculate profits, and build relationships with suppliers and customers. They needed to understand supply and demand."

"Excellent," the Professor affirmed. "The trader stage saw the development of primitive financial concepts like credit and debt. Trust was the foremost. This evolved into Commerce, the establishment of organized markets and trade routes. The arrival of foreign powers, as we discussed, brought both opportunities and challenges. Mythili, what financial lessons can we derive from the colonial era?"

Mythili's expression turned serious. "It highlighted the dangers of economic dependence. The exploitation of resources, the imposition of unfair trade practices, and the suppression of local industries demonstrated the importance of protecting economic sovereignty. It also showed the need for financial regulations to protect local businesses, and consumers."

"Indeed," Professor said. "This era also witnessed the emergence of formal financial institutions, like banks, and the use of standardized currencies. These developments facilitated larger-scale transactions and pulled economic growth. As we learned in our earlier discussion, the Guru judged that true economic progress was tied to social upliftment. He challenged the caste-based restrictions on trade, empowering marginalized communities to participate in the marketplace. Pavan, what financial impact did his teachings have?"

Pavan replied, "he created a more inclusive economy. By empowering more people to participate in trade and develop the market, he increased the overall wealth of the region. He also taught people to be self-reliant, which is a crucial financial skill."

"Perfectly," the Professor said. "Post-independence, Kerala witnessed the rise of a robust consumer market, fueled by the remittances from abroad, and improved infrastructure. This brings us to the present era of e-commerce. Mythili, what financial advantages does e-commerce offer to consumers and businesses?"

Mythili responded, "For consumers, it offers convenience, price transparency, and access to a wider range of products. For businesses, it reduces overhead costs, expands market reach, and provides valuable data on consumer behavior. It also allows for micro transactions, and the ability to operate a business with very low overhead."

"And what financial challenges does it present?" Professor sniggled.

Mythili continued, "It brings challenges like cybersecurity risks, the need for robust payment systems, and the potential for increased competition. It also requires a high level of digital literacy as well as financial literacy, and the ability to adapt to rapid technological changes."

"Precisely," Professor agreed. "Pavan, how can individuals and businesses steer the complexities of the digital economy, and what financial learnings can we gather from the rapid growth of online commerce?"

Pavan reacted, "We must prioritize digital literacy, learn about cybersecurity, and embrace data analytics. We need to understand the importance of building trust in online transactions, and the need for ethical e-commerce practices. We also need to understand the power of data, and how it can be used to make informed financial decisions. The text shows the large amount of money that is being transferred via these modes, and that we must understand how to protect ourselves, and our money."

"Excellent," Professor said. "Throughout this evolution, **several financial learnings have remained constant: the importance of understanding value, managing risk, building trust, and adapting to change**. But perhaps the most crucial lesson is the need for continuous learning and reinvention. As the Guru taught, knowledge is paramount to empowerment. In today's digital age, this means embracing lifelong learning, acquiring new skills, and adapting to the ever-changing landscape of commerce. We must never stop learning, and we must always be willing to reinvent ourselves. The future of trade is not just about technology; it is about human ingenuity, adaptability, and the relentless pursuit of knowledge. The Guru's advice to give equal emphasis to commerce and science, and technology, as envisaged in the eight topics for the Sivagiri Pilgrimage, requires special mention in this context."

Key Learnings from the current discussion can be condensed as:

- **Barter:** Limitations of direct exchange, need for a medium in determining the value of the products and services.
- **Trader:** Essential skills: negotiation, risk, resolving the value in the monetary units, basic accounting, trust, and creditworthiness.
- **Commerce:** Market impact, dangers of dependence, need for regulation, formal finance emerges, and inclusion increases the wealth.
- **E-commerce:** Convenience and reach vs. cybersecurity, digital literacy, data ethics.

Timeless Principles from the Guru

- **Value:** Discern true worth, make informed decisions.
- **Risk:** Prudent assessment, diversification, security, and protection.
- **Trust:** Ethical conduct, build strong relationships, secure transactions.
- **Adaptability:** Embrace change, learn, innovate.
- **Knowledge:** Lifelong learning = empowerment.
- **Protection:** Responsible stewardship, secure finances, digital safety.

13

Collective Strength: Joint Stock Companies for Growth

The Professor's chamber, usually a haven of quiet contemplation, had morphed into a vibrant stage, a theatre of economic history. Professor, a man whose passion for the subject was a palpable force, stood before his students, Mythili and Pavan, his eyes alight with the passion of a storyteller unveiling an ancient epic. The projector hummed, casting a warm, golden glow across the room, displaying a mesmerizing animation – a spiraling estuary of coins, gears, and miniature factories, symbolizing the dynamic magic of capital.

"Imagine," Professor began, his voice resounding with the rhythm of a seasoned orator, "a single, unassuming seed. It holds within it the potential for a majestic tree, a symbol of growth, strength, and enduring life. But without the nourishing embrace of fertile soil, the life-giving warmth of sunlight, and the quenching thirst of water, that potential remains locked, dormant, unrealized. Similarly, an entrepreneurial idea, a spark of innovation, no matter how brilliant, how revolutionary, withers and fades without the lifeblood of financial resources."

He gestured towards the animated diagram, where tiny coin icons, shimmering like golden fireflies, were flowing into a central, pulsating hub. "Today, we're not merely dissecting abstract financial concepts; we're witnessing the very essence of capital formation, the magic that transforms dreams into tangible realities. We're exploring how the Guru, a visionary far ahead of his time, understood the power of collective investment, the ability of a community to pool its resources and build a foundation for lasting prosperity."

Professor's voice softened, taking on a more intimate tone. "Let's begin with the seed money, the initial capital, the spark that ignites the engine of enterprise. In the ancient days, in the incipient stages of commerce, it was often the endeavor of a lone individual, a daring risk-taker, or perhaps a small, tightly knit partnership. But the Guru, with his profound understanding of human potential, saw a different path, a path of collective strength, a symphony of capital."

He paused, allowing the image of a bustling factory floor, alive with the rhythm of machinery and the energy of human endeavor, to flash across the screen. "Imagine a village, a community brimming with skilled artisans, their hands capable of making wonders, their minds alive with innovative ideas. But without the required tools, the machines that supplement their capabilities, the raw materials that fuel their creativity, their potential remains untapped, their talents languish. The Guru's solution, the joint stock company, was a revolutionary concept, a vessel for collective prosperity, a mechanism for transforming individual aspirations into shared achievements."

Professor Siva then delved into the intricacies of financing, painting vivid pictures with his words, transforming abstract concepts into tangible realities. "Think of equity financing as planting a shared orchard, a collective endeavor where each investor becomes a co-owner, sharing in the bountiful harvest of the company's labor. Debt financing, on the other hand, is like borrowing a cart for a long and arduous journey. You gain the means to travel, to transport your goods, but you must return the cart with the rent, after your journey is complete. In respect of borrowed money, interest is to be paid in lieu of rent besides principal amount."

He leaned forward, his eyes gleaming with the intensity of a master craftsman revealing a hidden technique. "Choosing the right financing strategy is related to selecting the perfect blend of spices for a culinary masterpiece. Too much debt, and your company becomes burdened, weighed down, unable to move with agility and grace. Too little equity, and you risk losing control of your creation, surrendering your vision to external forces. The Guru deduced this delicate balance, urging his followers to be both bold and prudent, to embrace calculated risks while maintaining a keen awareness of potential pitfalls."

The animated diagram now showcased the financial advantages of joint stock companies, each point illuminated with a brief, captivating story, a depiction of human ingenuity and collective achievement. "Imagine a small weaver, his hands skilled in the art of creating intricate fabrics, but hesitant to invest his meager savings, fearing personal wipe-out. But with the shield of limited liability, his risk is contained, and his confidence blossoms. He becomes a shareholder, a co-owner, contributing to a larger enterprise, sharing in its success, and witnessing his craft reach a wider audience."

The Professor then spoke of the power of perpetual existence, the enduring legacy of a company that excels in the lives of its individual founders. "Think of a company as a river, flowing continuously, its waters replenished by countless tributaries, unaffected by the ebb and flow of individual lives. Unlike a small pond, which can dry up in the face of adversity, a company, with its perpetual existence, ensures long-term stability, fostering growth and innovation across generations."

He painted a vivid picture of scalability, the ability of a company to expand its operations, to amplify its impact, to transform a small endeavor into a powerhouse of production. "Imagine a small workshop, its artisans struggling to meet the ever-growing demand for their handcrafted goods. But with the influx of capital from a multitude of shareholders, it expands, modernizes, embraces new technologies, and becomes a beacon of industrial progress. This is the magic of scalability, the ability to grow and adapt, to meet the challenges of a dynamic marketplace."

The Professor's voice took on a more passionate tone as he spoke of financial literacy, the cornerstone of Guru's vision for economic empowerment. "The Guru wasn't just building factories and workshops; he was building minds, cultivating a culture of financial awareness. He made out that financial literacy was the key to unlocking true empowerment, to liberating individuals from the shackles of economic dependence. He wanted his followers to understand the language of money, to make informed decisions, to be masters of their own destiny, to navigate the complexities of the marketplace with confidence and skill."

He then spotlighted the importance of transparency and accountability, the ethical foundation upon which a successful enterprise is built. "Imagine a company, open and honest, its financial records meticulously maintained, its operations guided by the principles of integrity and fairness. This builds trust, attracting investors, customers, and partners, creating a virtuous cycle of growth and prosperity. In the digital age, where information flows freely and reputations are built and shattered in an instant, this transparency is even more crucial, a testament to the company's commitment to ethical conduct."

Professor's voice resonated with conviction as he spoke of the enduring relevance of the Guru's vision. "The Guru's vision was not just about building companies; it was about building a community, a nation, empowered by collective prosperity. He kindled that financial strength was the foundation for social progress, the key to unlocking opportunities for all. By embracing the principles of joint stock companies, we can unlock the alchemy of capital, transforming dreams into tangible realities, building a more equitable and prosperous future for generations to come."

He then began to weave in the financial concepts with greater detail. "When the Guru advocated for Joint Stock Companies, he was advocating for a robust method of **Capital Formation**. This is the process where savings in an economy are mobilized and channeled into investments. He understood that individual savings, while important, were insufficient for large-scale industrial development. By pooling resources, a larger capital base could be formed. This allowed for projects that would have been impossible for individuals or small partnerships."

"This also brings in the concept of **Economies of Scale**. By increasing the scale of production, the cost per unit decreases. This is a crucial concept in manufacturing. Large-scale production requires large capital outlays, something that a Joint Stock Company can provide. The Guru wanted to bring the benefits of large-scale production to the community."

"The Guru's vision also encompassed the idea of **Risk Diversification**. In traditional business structures, risk was concentrated. If a business failed, the owner or partners would bear the full brunt of the losses. Joint Stock Companies, with their limited liability structure, spread the risk among a large number of shareholders. This allowed for investments in more ambitious projects, as the potential losses were mitigated."

"He also understood the importance of **Financial Instruments**. The ability to issue shares, debentures, and other long-term borrowings allowed companies to raise capital from a variety of sources. This flexibility was crucial for funding different stages of development. He wanted to bring this level of financial sophistication to the community, to empower them with the tools of modern finance."

"The Guru's teachings were not just about raising capital; they were about **Financial Management**. He advocated that capital had to be used efficiently and effectively. This included budgeting, forecasting, and controlling expenses. He wanted the community to be financially literate, to understand how to manage their limited resources wisely."

"The Guru also understood the importance of **Corporate Governance**. The separation of ownership and management in the Joint Stock Companies created the need for mechanisms to ensure that the company was run in the best interests of the shareholders. This included the appointment of independent directors, the establishment of audit committees, and the implementation of transparent reporting practices. The Guru's vision was ahead of its time in recognizing the importance of good governance."

"The Guru also recognized the power of **Dividends and Shareholder Value**. By sharing the profits of the company with the shareholders, companies could incentivize investment and build long-term relationships. He wanted to create a system where everyone could share in the prosperity created by industrial development."

"And finally, the Guru reminded the importance of **Long-term Investment**. He was not just interested in short-term gains; he wanted to build a sustainable industrial base for the community. This required a long-term perspective, a willingness to reinvest profits, and a commitment to continuous innovation. He wanted to instill a culture of long-term thinking, a culture of building for the future."

The Professor then began to bring in historical examples, making the abstract concepts tangible. He spoke of the Malabar Economic Union, founded by Dr. Palpu, the leader of the Yogam, a company that embodied the Guru's vision of collective enterprise. 'Imagine,' he said, 'a company that not only traded in coir and copra, but also fostered a spirit of economic independence. This was more than just a business; it was a symbol of empowerment, a testament to the potential of collective action.'

"He then recounted the story of the Thomas Stephen Company, founded by Kochera Panicker and Achutha Panicker, at Kollam, a pioneering Tile Factory that thrived under the Guru's blessings. 'This company,' Professor emphasized, 'demonstrated the power of combining technical expertise with spiritual guidance. It showed that industry and spirituality could coexist, that material progress and moral values were not mutually exclusive.'

The Professor then turned to the Union Tile Factory, established under the leadership of the great poet and the General Secretary of the Yogam, Kumaran Asan. "This company," he explained, "was a testament to the importance of meticulous financial management. Kumaran Asan, a poet and visionary, also possessed a keen understanding of accounting and finance. He personally oversaw the company's financial records, ensuring transparency and accountability."

The Professor then spoke of numerous other companies registered in Travancore, a testament to the transformative power of the Guru's teachings. 'These companies,' he said, 'were not just economic entities; they were agents of social change. They provided employment opportunities, fostered entrepreneurship, and challenged the traditional social order.

He then began to discuss the broader impact of the Guru's vision, highlighting the recognition it received from other communities and groups. The globally known communist and former chief minister, E.M.S. Namboothiripad's speech, the Professor explained, 'was a powerful acknowledgment of the Guru's foresight. He recognized that economic empowerment was essential for social progress, and he urged his own community to embrace the principles of trade and industry.'

The Professor then began to weave in the concept of **Financial Inclusion**, a concept that is very relevant today. ' The Guru's vision,' he explained, 'was inherently inclusive. He wanted to create an economy where everyone could participate, regardless of their social background. Joint Stock Companies provided a mechanism for small investors to participate in large-scale enterprises, democratizing access to capital.'

The Professor then discussed the importance of **Financial Innovation**. 'The Guru's advocacy for Joint Stock Companies was itself an act of financial innovation,' the Professor explained. ' The Guru recognized the limitations of traditional business structures and sought to create a new model that would be more conducive to industrial development. Today, we need to continue this spirit of innovation, developing new financial instruments and models to meet the challenges of a rapidly changing economy.'

The Professor then spoke of the importance of **Financial Regulation**. 'While the Guru advocated for economic freedom, he also understood the importance of protecting investors and ensuring fair competition,' he explained. 'This requires a robust regulatory framework, one that balances the need for innovation with the need for investor protection. Today, we need to strengthen our regulatory framework to address the challenges of the digital economy.'

He then began to discuss the concept of **Sustainable Development**. 'The Guru's vision was not just about economic growth; it was about sustainable development,' the Professor explained. 'He wanted to create an economy that would benefit future generations. This requires a focus on environmental protection, social responsibility, and ethical business practices. Today, we need to integrate these principles into our financial decision-making.'

He then spoke of the importance of **Financial Education**. ' The Guru taught that knowledge was the key to empowerment,' he explained. 'He wanted his followers to be financially literate, to understand how to manage their resources wisely. Today, we need to expand access to financial education, particularly for underserved communities.'

The Professor then began to highlight the role of **Technology in Finance**. 'The Guru's vision was ahead of its time, but today, we have the tools to realize his vision on a much larger scale,' he explained. ' Technology can democratize access to financial services, reduce transaction costs, and enhance transparency. We need to embrace these technologies, while also being mindful of the potential risks.'

He then spoke of the importance of **Global Financial Integration**. 'The Guru recognized the importance of international trade and investment,' he explained. 'Today, we live in a globalized economy, where capital flows freely across borders. We need to understand the dynamics of global finance, and we need to develop strategies to attract foreign investment and promote exports.'

The Professor then began to discuss the concept of **Financial Resilience**. 'The Guru's vision was about building a strong and resilient economy,' he explained. 'This requires a diversified economy, a robust financial system, and a culture of entrepreneurship. Today, we need to strengthen our financial resilience to withstand economic shocks and crises.

He then began to highlight the importance of **Ethical Leadership in Finance**. 'The Guru's teachings were rooted in ethical principles,' he explained. 'He wanted his followers to conduct business with integrity and fairness. Today, we need to promote ethical leadership in finance, ensuring that financial institutions and businesses operate in a responsible and sustainable manner.'

The Professor then concluded his lecture with a powerful message of hope and inspiration. 'The Guru's vision,' he said, 'was not just a dream; it was a blueprint for a better future. By embracing his principles of collective action, financial literacy, and ethical conduct, we can build a more just and prosperous society for all.'

The Professor's Chamber, now bathed in the warm glow of the projector, was filled with a sense of awe and inspiration. Mythili and Pavan, their minds ignited by Professor Siva's narrative, had witnessed the transformative power of the Guru's vision, a legacy that continues to shape the economic landscape of Kerala and beyond.

The key Learnings in the current day's discussion were displayed by the Professor on the screen:

- **Collective Capital:** Pooling resources enables large-scale industrial growth.
- **Economies of Scale:** Increased production drives efficiency and lowers costs.
- **Risk Diversification:** Limited liability spreads risk, encouraging investment.
- **Financial Tools:** Utilizing diverse instruments (shares, bonds) for capital raising.
- **Sound Management:** Financial literacy and efficient resource use are crucial.
- **Good Governance:** Transparency and accountability protect shareholder interests.
- **Shared Prosperity:** Dividends and long-term investment build shared wealth.
- **Ethical and sustainable growth**: Combining financial success with integrity and long-term vision.

14

The Cooperative Way: Empowering Communities through Collaboration

The Professor's Chamber was no longer a mere room — it was a sanctuary of shadows and light, its walls softened by the amber flicker of a projector's beam. Rows of desks had been swept aside, replaced by a crescent of chairs that curved like the embrace of an ancient council. Mythili settled on the edge of her seat, her dark braid swaying as she leaned forward, her sharp eyes drinking in the scene. Beside her, Pavan dragged slightly, his fingers drumming a restless rhythm on his knee, though his gaze betrayed a hunger for what was to come. At the circle's heart stood Professor Siva, a figure carved from quiet intensity — his silver hair catching the light, his voice a low tide ready to swell.

"Close your eyes," he began, his words unfurling like smoke, curling into the stillness. "Imagine a village cradled in the arms of emerald hills, where the dawn spills molten gold across fields of swaying millet. Farmers rise with the first rooster's cry, their backs bent beneath the sun's unrelenting gaze, their hands rough as the earth they till. Their harvests are scant — grains slipping through cracked fingers, dreams withering like seedlings in a drought. Each stands alone, a solitary shadow against the vastness, their voices lost to the wind. But then — a murmur stirs. A spark catches. A whisper ripples through the dust: **"What if we stood together?"**

The Professor's hand swept toward the screen, and light erupted into motion. Five vivid figures bloomed from the glow, each a brushstroke of life: a lone craftsman, his hammer ringing against an anvil under a sagging roof; two merchants, their voices clashing like swords in a spice-dusted bazaar; a throng of shareholders, their suits crisp as they murmured in a glass-walled tower; a knot of villagers, their laughter rising around a crackling fire; and a stern government hall, its pillars cold and unyielding. "These," he declared, his voice surging with the weight of revelation, "are the five threads of our economic tapestry: the solitary soul, the partnered pursuit, the corporate chorus, the united hearth, and the guiding state. Tonight, we plunge into the fourth — the cooperative — a constellation of wills forged into a single, radiant flame."

His tone dipped, reverent as a prayer, as he summoned a name that seemed to hum in the air: "The Guru was no ordinary man — he was a seer, his eyes piercing the fog of despair that cloaked his people. In Kerala's villages, where poverty chained souls to the ground, he saw not brokenness but possibility. 'Organize and become strong,' he whispered, his words a seed cast into fertile earth. And from that seed sprang a revolution — not of swords, but of hands clasped in purpose. Markets bloomed where silence once reigned, children ran where hunger once prowled. The Guru's vision reshaped the land, a testament to the quiet might of unity."

The screen flared with life: a market unfurled in riotous color — stalls groaning under pyramids of rice and saffron, women in bright saris bartering with sharp tongues, children weaving through the throng with sticky mango-stained grins. "The word 'cooperate' — from the Latin

cooperari, 'to work as one' — is no dusty relic," Professor said, his voice threading the scene with meaning. "It is a living pulse, a tapestry stitched from shared dreams, where every thread strengthens the whole. It is the Guru's call made flesh — a chorus of voices rising where once there was only silence."

He stepped closer, his stories glowing like lotus flowers on a still pond. "Picture farmers, their fields golden but their pockets empty, their harvests snatched by middlemen with vulture smiles. The rice they bled for feeds distant tables, leaving their own children hollow-eyed. Then, they awaken. A cooperative forms, a pact sealed under a mango tree's shade. They pool their grain, bypass the predators, and sell directly to the hungry. Profits flow back to calloused hands, chains of exploitation snap like dry twigs. This is a **united effort** — a river bursting through a brittle dam, unstoppable."

"See a village lashed by a monsoon's wrath — roofs torn away like paper, fields drowned in a sea of mud. A widow clutches her last sack of lentils, a father stares at his shattered loom. Despair looms, heavy as the storm clouds. Yet they do not rot. They gather beneath a leaking tarp, sharing their scraps — lentils, rice, a half-rotted yam. Together, they hoist beams, patch roofs, and coax life back into the soaked earth. This is **mutual assistance** — a phoenix clawing free from ash, wings spread wide."

"Imagine a meeting beneath a banyan tree, its roots sprawling like the veins of the village itself. Old men with weathered faces sit beside young women with fire in their eyes, the rich beside the ragged. Every voice rises — sharp, soft, trembling, bold — each heard, each equal. Decisions warm in the crucible of debate, leadership forged not by force but by the slow burn of consensus. This is **leadership through consensus** — the heartbeat of democracy, steady and alive."

Professor's gaze lifted, his tale stretching across oceans and centuries. "In London, a grand hall pulses with life — delegates from every corner of the earth, their tongues a symphony of struggle and triumph. A fisherman from Japan trades tales with a weaver from Peru, a dairyman from Denmark nods to a farmer from Kenya. This is the International Cooperative Alliance — the ICA — a lighthouse blazing through the fog of division, proving unity is no dream but a force that spans the globe."

He paused, hands tracing invisible threads as he unveiled the seven principles of cooperation, each a parable carved in light. "Envision a village gate flung wide, its rusted hinges creaking an invitation. A beggar with tattered shoes steps through beside a merchant with silk robes — no questions, no scorn. This is **voluntary membership** — a door open to all who choose to walk in."

"See a circle of faces beneath a flickering lantern, each with one vote — neither good nor lineage tips the scales. A widow's whisper carries the weight of a landlord's shout. This is **democratic governance** — equality's fierce, unyielding hymn."

"Picture a harvest divided not by greed but by toil — every sickle, every sweat-drop counted. A boy who hauled water shares the bounty with the woman who reaped the stalks. This is **economic participation** — justice ripened into grain."

"Imagine a cooperative standing tall, its roots deep, its course charted by its own stars — no distant tyrant pulls its strings. This is a **self-governing community** — autonomy's quiet thunder."

"See a courtyard alive with learning — elders teaching the rhythm of the loom, youths scribbling numbers in the dust, a girl tracing maps of trade routes. Knowledge flows like a river, free to all. This is **space for knowledge acquisition** — growth as a sacred vow."

"Envision cooperatives clasping hands across borders — a fisherman's net mended by a tailor's thread, a farmer's rice sold in a weaver's market. A web of strength spans continents. This is **coexistence with others** — a kinship that knows no horizon."

"Picture a village reborn — wells bubbling with clean water, children plump with rice and milk, streets ringing with trade and song. The cooperative tends its own, a gardener to its soil. This is a **concern for the community** — a heart beating for every soul within its reach."

The screen dimmed, then flared with shadows of a harsher age. "Journey back to Britain's industrial abyss," Professor intoned, his voice a blade cutting through time. "Smokestacks claw the sky, engraving residue that chokes the lungs of children toiling for sixteen hours for a crust of bread. Workers are cogs in a machine of greed, their lives ground to dust. Yet in this darkness, a flame flickers — a rebellion clad not in steel but in hope. The cooperative is born."

He conjured Robert Owen, a dreamer with a voice like rolling thunder, and the Rochdale Pioneers, weavers with hunger in their bellies and fire in their fists. "See them — ragged, unshaven, their hands cracked from looms — gathering in a damp cellar. They scrape together pennies; open a store where scales weigh true, where bread isn't laced with chalk. The Rochdale Society rises — an ember glowing in a coal-black night, a promise that fairness can outlast despair."

The tale spiraled onward, threading through continents and creeds. "In Britain, Christian socialists kneel in candlelit chapels, dreaming of a world remade by love and mutual aid — a gospel of cooperation. In America, the Grover movement sweeps the plains, arming farmers with seed and savvy, a shield against the wolves of the market. In Soviet Russia, cooperatives became bricks in a socialist dawn, lifting peasants from mud to mastery, a creed of collective might."

Then, to India — a land of dust and divinity. "See Sir Frederick Nicholson, his coat dusty from rutted roads, his eyes tracing the veins of a nation bowed by want. He plants cooperatives like saplings, their roots cracking the stone of poverty. See Pandit Nehru, his jaw set, his mind ablaze with a vision — a nation stitched by unity, education, and shared purpose, a fabric to cradle a billion dreams."

The Professor's voice turned homeward, to Kerala's sun-drenched shores. "Imagine the Guru, a quiet giant in a white *mundu*, standing on a hillock as the sea roars below. He sees his people — fishermen with empty nets, farmers with barren fields, women with no voice — and his heart aches. He lights the spark. Credit cooperatives bloom, coins clinking into farmers' hands for seeds and struggles. Marketing cooperatives carry artisans' wares — brass lamps, woven mats — to distant markets. Consumer cooperatives break the stranglehold of profiteers, rice is sold at prices that don't bite. Storage cooperatives shield harvests from monsoon rot, a bulwark against fate. Self-help groups rise — women with henna-stained hands pooling rupees, weaving futures from threads of microfinance."

He wove in the torchbearers of the Guru's flame. "Picture C. Krishnan, his voice a whip crack, rallying the casteless to claim their share. See T.K. Madhavan, his pen dripping ink like blood, carving justice into history's page. Watch Kerala's cooperatives gleam like gold — credit flowing like rivers, markets humming like hives, risks tamed by shared hands, voices rising in a chorus that shakes the sky."

The projector faded; its hum swallowed by silence. Mythili's breath caught; her fingers clenched around her bent. Pavan sat up right now, his drumming stilled, his eyes distant as if tracing the hills of that first village. Before them hung not just a lesson, but a saga — a flame of unity passed from the Guru's hands through centuries, across oceans, into their own shivering palms. Professor Siva stepped back, his shadow merging with the dark, leaving them to wrestle with the weight of it all: a call to weave their threads into the endless, radiant tapestry of cooperation.

Key Learnings from the present discussion were condensed by Professor Siva as:

- ***Diverse Enterprise Types:*** *The text identifies five main types of enterprises based on ownership: sole proprietorship, partnership, joint stock company, cooperative society, and public sector enterprise.*
- ***The Guru's vision on Cooperation:*** *Cooperatives played a crucial role in popularizing the concept of cooperative movement in Kerala, advocating for the establishment, to address socio-economic challenges.*
- ***Cooperative Principles:*** *The core principles of cooperative societies include united effort, mutual assistance, and consensus-based leadership, transcending social divisions.*
- ***International Cooperative Movement:*** *The International Cooperative Alliance (ICA) has been instrumental in standardizing and promoting cooperative principles globally.*
- ***Cooperative Benefits:*** *Cooperative enterprises aim to equitably distribute benefits, eliminate middleman exploitation, provide quality products/services, and improve members' living conditions.*
- ***Historical Context:*** *The cooperative movement emerged in response to the socio-economic imbalances caused by the Industrial Revolution, with variations in its development across different countries (Britain, USA, Russia).*

❖ ❖ ❖

15

Funding the Future: Banks and Entrepreneurial Support

The University gardens, a verdant sanctuary within the bustling campus, offered Mythili and Pavan a tranquil escape. Sunlight dappled through the canopy of ancient trees, casting dancing shadows on the winding paths as they strolled, their conversation weaving through the intricate tapestry of India's economic history.

"Imagine," Mythili began, her voice echoing the gentle rustle of leaves, "a world where financial institutions were the exclusive preserve of the elite, where the common man's dreams were shackled by the lack of access to capital."

Pavan nodded, his gaze sweeping across the manicured lawns. "It's hard to remeasure, isn't it? Today, we take banking for granted, but back then, it was a luxury, a distant dream for the common man. "

Their path led them to a quiet corner, where a stone bench offered a moment of respite. "Think about it," Pavan continued, "the very lifeblood of any enterprise, be it a modest shop or a sprawling factory, is finance. And in a developing nation like India, where capital was scarce, the role of banks was predominant. "

He recounted the history of Indian banking, a narrative punctuated by both promise and peril. The early days, marked by the rise and fall of institutions, often marred by malpractice and serving only the privileged few. The post-independence era witnessing a gradual transformation, a slow but steady democratization of financial services in the county.

The Professor mentioned the Bank of Hindustan (1760), the General Bank of India (1786), and the later established Banks of Bengal, Bombay, and Madras, highlighting the struggles and malpractices that plagued many of the early institutions. "Over 600 banks were established between 1760 and 1947, yet most were short-lived and served only specific princely states," he emphasized.

"The Reserve Bank of India," Mythili interjected, "the guardian of India's financial system, ensuring stability and accessibility. Public, private, foreign, cooperative, regional rural banks—a diverse ecosystem, all working towards the nation's economic progress. Public sector banks holding over 51 percent government shares, dominating 75 percent of Indian banking business, private sector banks owned by individuals, foreign banks operating under both Indian and their home country's regulations, cooperative banks at various levels, and regional rural banks established since 1975 to expand rural credit."

"But it wasn't always this way," Pavan reminded her, his voice imbued with a sense of wonder. "And that's where the Guru's vision becomes truly outstanding. In 1921, when the concept of banking was still alien to the masses, the Guru foresaw the need for a financial institution that would empower the common man."

The Professor then recounted the story of Swami Bodhananda, a man of unwavering dedication, a disciple who embodied the Guru's ideals. Once a force of fiery social reform, leading the Dharmabhata Sangha, he had found a new path, a path of spiritual enlightenment and social upliftment, under the Guru's guidance. "Before joining the Guru, Swami Bodhananda had formed the Dharmabhada Sangam in Cochin, and its members formed a core part of the workforce in establishing the bank."

"Bodhananda Swami faced a daunting challenge," Mythili murmured, her eyes reflecting the sunlight filtering through the leaves. "The economic landscape was bleak, the people impoverished, and financial institutions were inaccessible. Yet, the Guru's advice echoed in his mind: 'Money is lying around in this country. Is it not possible to collect it and utilize it properly? Think about what can be done with it.' "

Pavan painted the scene explicitly: Bodhananda Swami, seeking the Guru's blessing at Aluva Advaita Ashram, pouring out his concerns about the financial hardships faced by the people, especially the inability to gather resources for enterprise. The Guru's simple yet profound suggestion: "Why don't you think about starting a bank under the Companies Act?"

"Imagine the audacity of that vision," Pavan exclaimed, his voice filled with admiration. "To establish a bank, a formal financial institution, when the very concept was foreign to most. And not just any bank, but one that would serve the needs of the common man, the backbone of the society."

He described the monumental task that lay ahead: raising **ten lakh rupees**, a staggering sum in those days, equivalent to thousands of crores in today's terms based on the price of gold. It was decided at a meeting held in Koorkanchery, Thrissur, in 1921 that Shares would be issued at **fifty rupees** each for raising the initial capital for establishing a bank.

Bodhananda Swami, undeterred, embarked on a mission, fueled by the Guru's blessings and the unwavering support of the Dharmabhata Sangha. "The scarcity of financial resources was a major challenge, as most of the Guru's followers were economically disadvantaged. The existing banks were inaccessible to the common people."

"The story of Bodhananda Swami is a testament to the power of unwavering dedication," Mythili said, her voice filled with admiration. "His past, filled with revolutionary fervor, transformed into a force for constructive change under the Guru's guidance. He was born in 1883, travelled extensively, and was initiated as Bodhananda Giri by Iswarananda Mandaleshwar in Ujjain. He spent 20 years as the Guru's disciple after surrendering to him in 1908 at Thalassery."

Pavan nodded, his gaze fixed on the distant horizon. "He was a man of action, a visionary who translated the Guru's ideals into a physical reality. He understood the importance of financial inclusion, the need to empower the masses with access to credit and banking services."

He then recounted the meticulous planning, the preparation of bylaws, the attention to detail, all done in strict adherence to the Guru's instructions. The Guru suggested a system to overhaul existing banking systems, focusing on educating middle and lower-income groups about banking and providing maximum service to depositors and borrowers.

"And then," Pavan continued, his voice filled with a sense of awe, "came the intervention of the King of Cochin, a testament to the respect and reverence he held for The Guru. The bank was registered in 1921. Normally, a financial institution with a capital of ten lakh rupees would have paid a fee of **Rs. 500** for registration under the Companies Act. However, a Royal Decree waived the fee, and only **Rs. 75** was paid for office expenses. This unusual concession is a clear proof of the Royal family's respect for Sree Narayana Guru."

The establishment of the Cochin National Bank, a milestone in the annals of Indian banking, a testament to the transformative power of the Guru's vision, and the unwavering dedication of Swami Bodhananda. It was more than just a bank; it was a symbol of empowerment, a spotlight of hope for the common man, enabling "wealth and prosperity through industry," as the Guru advised.

"The Guru's legacy," Mythili articulated, her voice filled with emotion, "extends far beyond spiritual enlightenment. It contains social reform, economic empowerment, and a deep understanding of the human posture. He saw the potential in every individual, the power of collective action, and the importance of financial inclusion."

As they walked on, the sunlight streaming through the leaves, their conversation echoed through the serene gardens, a reminder of the enduring legacy of a visionary who dared to dream of a more equitable and prosperous society, diligently built with financial understanding.

Key Learnings from the discussions based on the descriptions in the main text were outlined by Pavan as:

- ***Financial Inclusion as a Catalyst:*** *Access to financial resources is critical for individual and economic empowerment, particularly in developing economies.*
- ***Historical Banking Limitations:*** *Early Indian banking was largely exclusive, plagued by malpractices, and inaccessible to the majority of the population.*
- ***Vision Accessible Banking:*** *Sree Narayana, the Guru, recognized the need for a bank to serve the common person, envisioning a financial institution that would uplift the economically disadvantaged.*
- ***Swami Bodhananda's role:*** *Swami Bodhananda played a vital role in translating the Guru's vision into a reality by establishing the Cochin National Bank, overcoming significant financial and logistical challenges.*

- ***Impact and Purpose of the Bank:*** *The Cochin National Bank aimed to democratize banking by educating and serving middle and lower-income groups, thereby revolutionizing financial accessibility.*
- ***Current Regulatory Framework:*** *The Reserve Bank of India (RBI) plays a pivotal role in regulating the modern Indian banking sector, which comprises diverse categories of banks to serve various economic needs of the mass.*

❖ ❖ ❖

16

The Guru's Legacy: Financial Institutions for the People

The Professor's Chamber, a haven of intellectual curiosity, buzzed with an almost palpable energy. Professor Siva, a man whose eyes held the wisdom of countless stories, settled into his usual spot, the worn wooden table· a silent witness to countless discussions. Mythili, her notebook open and pen poised, and Pavan, his brow furrowed in eager anticipation, mirrored his enthusiasm. Today's topic, the financial legacy of the Guru, promised to be a journey into uncharted territories, a glimpse into a world where banking transcended mere monetary transactions.

"Imagine," Professor began, his voice a gentle love, "a time when the very concept of a bank was masked in exclusivity, a privilege reserved for the elite. Picture a society where the vast majority were excluded from the very mechanisms designed to facilitate economic progress."

Mythili, her gaze fixed on the Professor, pondered the stark contrast. "It's almost unimaginable, Professor. We take for granted the accessibility of banking services today, the common presence of ATMs, the ease of online transactions."

"Indeed," Professor affirmed, his eyes tracing the intricate patterns on the wooden table. "But the Guru, with his profound understanding of human nature and his unwavering commitment to social upliftment, recognized the transformative potential of inclusive banking long before it became a mainstream concept. He saw beyond the traditional role of financial institutions, envisioning them as catalysts for social change, empowering the downtrodden and triggering economic growth from the grassroots."

Pavan, ever the realist, leaned forward, his curiosity outraged. "But how did the Guru translate this visionary idea into concrete action? How did he bridge the gap between abstract ideals and practical fulfilment?"

Professor's lips curved into a warm smile, a hint of admiration in his eyes. "The Guru's approach was nothing short of revolutionary. He championed the concept of 'social banking,' a paradigm shift where financial institutions would transcend their conventional role as profit-making entities and actively contribute to the well-being of society. He understood that true wealth was not merely about accumulating capital but about nurturing a society where everyone had the opportunity to thrive."

He paused, allowing his words to resound, then began to recount the story of the Cochin National Bank, established in 1921 under the Guru's guidance. "Imagine a bank," he said, his voice imbued with a sense of wonder, "that went beyond the mundane functions of accepting deposits and granting loans. Picture an institution that also provided financial support for students pursuing higher education, established hostels for the poor, created libraries to foster a culture of learning, and even offered assistance for the marriages of young women facing financial hardship."

Mythili's eyes widened; her imagination ignited by the sheer audacity of the concept. "That's extraordinary! It sounds like a forerunner to modern microfinance initiatives, a holistic approach to community development."

"Precisely," Professor affirmed, his voice filled with quiet satisfaction. "The Guru's ideas were decades ahead of their time. He comprehended that the financial institutions could be powerful instruments for social change, empowering individuals and communities to break free from the shackles of poverty and inequality. He saw the interconnectedness of economic well-being and social progress, recognizing that true prosperity could only be achieved when everyone had the opportunity to participate in the economic system."

He then delved into the bank's innovative approach to lending, a testament to the Guru's commitment to fairness and equity. "The Cochin National Bank implemented a differential interest rate system, offering lower rates to low-income individuals. This was a groundbreaking concept, challenging the conventional notion that access to credit should be determined by wealth and privilege. The Guru believed that everyone, regardless of their economic background, deserved a chance to build a better future."

Pavan, his brow sloped in thought, nodded thoughtfully. "It's remarkable how the Guru's ideas anticipated the principles of modern social banking. He deduced that financial inclusion was not just about providing access to banking services but also about ensuring affordability and fairness. He recognized that interest rates could be a significant barrier for those struggling to make both ends meet, and he sought to create a system that was more equitable and just."

The Professor then turned to the bank's operational model, highlighting its unique approach to capital mobilization. "The bank raised capital by issuing shares, with the first share symbolically held by 'Sree Narayana Guru resting in the Aluva Advaita Ashram.' This gesture was a powerful symbol of the Guru's enduring legacy and the bank's unwavering commitment to his ideals. It underscored the fact that the bank was not merely a commercial enterprise but a vehicle for social transformation, guided by the principles of compassion and service."

Professor also emphasized the bank's expansion efforts, illustrating its commitment to reaching out to underserved communities. "The bank, headquartered in Thrissur, shortly opened branches in Thriprayar and Valappad, extending its reach and impact. This expansion was not driven by a desire for profit maximization but by a genuine commitment to serving the needs of the community, bringing financial services to those who had been traditionally excluded."

However, Professor's voice took on a dimmed tone as he recounted the bank's eventual closure, a poignant reminder of the fragility of even the most well-intentioned initiatives. "The unexpected demise of Bodhananda Swami, the driving force behind the bank, in 1928 left a void in leadership, leading to its eventual cessation. It was a tragic loss, a setback in the journey towards financial inclusion."

Mythili's face fell, her empathy evident in her expression. "That's such a tragedy. It's a stark reminder that even the most visionary initiatives can be vulnerable without strong leadership and effective succession planning. It highlights the significance of building sustainable institutions that can withstand the challenges of time."

"Indeed," Professor agreed, his voice pigmented with a hint of melancholy. "But the legacy of the Cochin National Bank lives on. It served as a beacon of hope, demonstrating the transformative potential of social banking. It showed that financial institutions could be more than just repositories of wealth; they could be catalysts for social change, empowering individuals and communities to build a brighter future."

Professor then shifted the focus to other banking institutions inspired by the Guru's vision, highlighting the enduring impact of his ideas. "Although the Cochin National Bank could not sustain, the Guru's ideas continued to inspire others, igniting a spark of social entrepreneurship that would transform the landscape of Indian banking. Two notable examples are the Bharat Bank and the Sree Narayana Guru Cooperative Bank, both established in Mumbai, far from the geographical heart of the Guru's activities."

Pavan's eyes lit up, his interest piqued by the mention of Bharat Bank. "I've heard of Bharat Bank! It's one of the leading cooperative banks in the country, known for its strong focus on financial inclusion and its commitment to serving the needs of marginalized communities."

"Exactly," Professor confirmed, his voice filled with quiet satisfaction. " Founded by members of the Billava community, inspired by the teachings of the great Guru. Bharat Bank has grown from a small cooperative to a multi-state institution with over a hundred branches and an annual turnover of INR 18,000 crore. It's a testament to the power of collective action and the enduring relevance of the Guru's vision. It demonstrates that even small communities, united by a common purpose and guided by the principles of compassion and service, can achieve remarkable things."

He then delved into the history of Bharat Bank, tracing its roots to the vision of the Guru. "The founders of Bharat Bank, many of whom had migrated to Mumbai in search of better opportunities, were deeply inspired by the Guru's teachings in their teenage years. They saw in his philosophy a blueprint for building a more equitable and just society, a society where everyone had the opportunity to prosper."

"They recognized the importance of financial inclusion as a tool for empowerment, and they sought to create a banking institution that would serve the needs of their community, providing access to credit and financial services to those who had been traditionally excluded. They understood that financial empowerment was not just about providing access to capital but also about fostering a sense of ownership and responsibility, empowering individuals to take control of their economic destinies."

He also highlighted the bank's commitment to social responsibility, emphasizing its role as a catalyst for community development. "Bharat Bank has consistently demonstrated its commitment to social responsibility, supporting various initiatives aimed at improving the lives of marginalized communities. It has invested in education, healthcare, and infrastructure development, recognizing that true prosperity can only be achieved when everyone has the opportunity to thrive."

Professor then spoke of the Sree Narayana Guru Cooperative Bank, another testament to the enduring influence of the Guru's vision. "The Sree Narayana Guru Cooperative Bank, established by the Keralites in Mumbai, is another example of a financial institution guided by the principles of compassion and service. It provides financial services to its members, cultivating a sense of community and promoting economic empowerment."

He emphasized the bank's commitment to serving its members, highlighting its role as a trusted financial partner. "The bank has built a strong reputation for its personalized service and its commitment to understanding the unique needs of its members. It has encouraged a sense of trust and community, creating a supportive environment where members feel valued and respected."

Professor concluded the chapter by emphasizing the broader impact of the Guru's vision on the Indian banking landscape. "The Guru's ideas on social banking were not merely abstract concepts; they translated into tangible institutions that empowered individuals and communities, transforming the landscape of Indian banking. His legacy continues to inspire us to build a financial system that is inclusive, equitable, and that truly serves the needs of all."

"The Guru's vision," Professor continued, his voice echoing with a quiet intensity "was not confined to the mere establishment of financial institutions. He sought to instill a fundamental shift in the very ethos of banking, a transition from a system driven by profit to one infused with compassion and social responsibility."

He paused, allowing his words to sink in, then elaborated, "He envisioned a banking system that would act as a catalyst for social transformation, a system that would not only provide access to credit and financial services but also foster a sense of empowerment and dignity among the marginalized. He believed that true economic progress could only be achieved when everyone had the opportunity to participate in the system, to contribute their talents and skills, and to share in the fruits of their labor."

Mythili, her brow furrowed in thought, asked, "Professor, how did the Guru's vision differ from the prevailing banking practices of his time? What were the key elements that distinguished his approach?"

Professor smiled, acknowledging her insightful question. "That's a crucial point, Mythili. The banking system of the Guru's era was largely characterized by exclusivity and elitism. It was a system that broadened to the needs of the wealthy and powerful, while neglecting most of the population. Access to credit was determined by social status and economic privilege, creating a system of deep-rooted inequality."

He then elaborated on the key elements of the Guru's approach. "The Guru's vision was fundamentally different. He sought to normalize access to finance, to break down the barriers that excluded the marginalized, and to create a system that was inclusive and equitable. He focused on the importance of social responsibility, urging financial institutions to go beyond their traditional role as profit-making entities and to actively contribute to the well-being of society."

"One of the key elements of his approach was the emphasis on differential interest rates," he continued. "The Guru recognized that interest rates could be a significant barrier for low-income individuals, and he sought to create a system that was more affordable and accessible. He also stressed the importance of providing financial literacy and education, empowering individuals to make informed financial decisions and to manage their resources effectively."

Pavan, his pragmatic mind grappling with the complexities of the subject, asked, "Professor, how did the Guru's vision address the issue of financial risk? How did he balance the need for social responsibility with the need for financial sustainability?"

Professor nodded, acknowledging the validity of his question. "That's a crucial consideration, Pavan. The Guru realized that financial institutions had a responsibility to manage risk judiciously. He regarded the importance of sound financial management and prudent lending practices. However, he also believed that risk assessment should not be solely based on traditional financial metrics. He urged financial institutions to consider the social impact of their lending decisions, to assess the potential for positive social change, and to support initiatives that would create long-term economic and social benefits."

Professor then elaborated on the practical aspects of the Guru's approach. "The Guru's vision was not about dispensing charity or engaging in reckless lending. It was about creating a system that would empower individuals to become self-reliant and to contribute to the economic development of their communities. He emphasized the importance of providing access to training and skills development, enabling individuals to start their own businesses and to generate sustainable income."

"The Guru also accented the importance of building strong community-based institutions," he continued. "He believed that local communities were best positioned to understand their own needs and to develop solutions that were tailored to their specific circumstances. He encouraged the formation of cooperative societies and other community-based organizations, empowering individuals to pool their resources and to work together to achieve common goals."

The Professor then returned to the narrative of the Bharat Bank, highlighting its remarkable growth and its enduring commitment to the Guru's vision. "The Bharat Bank," he said, "is a testament to the power of the Guru's ideas. It has grown from a small cooperative to a multi-state institution, providing access to financial services to millions of people. Its success is a reflection of its commitment to social responsibility, its focus on financial inclusion, and its unwavering adherence to the principles of compassion and service."

He then shared episodes illustrating the bank's commitment to social responsibility. "The bank has supported numerous initiatives aimed at improving the lives of marginalized communities," he said. "It has provided scholarships to students from underprivileged backgrounds, funded the construction of schools and hospitals, and supported programs that promote entrepreneurship and economic development."

"It has also played a crucial role in promoting financial literacy and education," he continued. "It has conducted workshops and seminars to educate people about financial management, helping them to make informed decisions and to build a secure financial future."

Professor then shifted his focus to the Sree Narayana Guru Cooperative Bank, highlighting its role in serving the needs of the Malayali community in Mumbai. "The Sree Narayana Guru Cooperative Bank," he said, "is another example of a financial institution guided by the principles of the

Guru's vision. It provides financial services to its members, furthering a sense of community and promoting economic empowerment."

Professor then shared stories of the bank's impact on its members. "The bank has helped many individuals to start their own businesses, to purchase homes, and to send their children to school," he said. "It has provided a lifeline for those who have been excluded from the mainstream financial system, giving them the opportunity to build a better future."

"It has also played a crucial role in preserving the cultural heritage of the Malayali community," he continued. "It has supported cultural events and initiatives, fostering a sense of identity and belonging among its members."

Professor concluded the discussions by emphasizing the enduring relevance of the Guru's vision in the contemporary world. "The Guru's ideas on social banking are more relevant than ever," he said. "In a world where inequality is rampant and financial exclusion is a major challenge; his vision offers a blueprint for building a more just and equitable society. It reminds us that financial institutions can be powerful instruments for social change, catalysts for empowerment and progress."

"The Guru's legacy challenges us to rethink the very purpose of banking," he continued. "It urges us to move beyond the narrow focus on profit maximization and to embrace a broader vision of social responsibility. It calls upon us to create a financial system that is not only efficient and profitable but also compassionate and inclusive."

"The Guru's vision," he concluded, his voice filled with quiet conviction, "is a beacon of hope in a world that often seems driven by greed and self-interest. It reminds us that true wealth is not merely about accumulating material possessions but about building a society where everyone has the opportunity to thrive, where compassion and service are the guiding principles, and where the silent currency of kindness and empathy flows freely."

Key Learnings of the brave discussion on the current topic were condensed by the Professor as:

- ***The Guru's Vision of Equitable Banking:*** *He championed banking for the marginalized, leading to the innovative Cochin National Bank with social objectives like student aid and low-interest loans, predating modern social banking.*
- ***Cochin National Bank's Impact:*** *Founded by Swami Bodhananda, it pioneered differential interest rates, but his sudden death led to its closure, despite its positive impact on education and small businesses.*
- ***The success of Bharat Bank:*** *Founded in Mumbai, it thrived as a multi-state cooperative bank, directly attributing its success to the Guru's teachings and serving all communities.*
- ***The Sree Narayana Guru Cooperative Bank:*** *Another Mumbai-based bank, established by the Keralites, showcases the Guru's lasting influence on cooperative banking, with consistent growth and modern services.*
- ***Kerala's Cooperative Banking Movement:*** *The Guru's influence sparked the growth of cooperative societies and banks in Kerala, including the pioneering Calicut Bank (C. Krishnan), and was expanded by T.K.Madhavan, empowering diverse sectors and marginalized communities.*
- ***Empowerment and Social Change:*** *These banking institutions, especially in Kerala, played a vital role in empowering historically marginalized communities, fostering economic development, and embodying the Guru's vision of social upliftment.*

❖ ❖ ❖

17

Harmony in Action: Cooperation between Employees and Management

The Professor's chamber, a sanctuary of shared knowledge, held a peaceful anticipation. Professor Siva, his bearing a blend of scholarly rigor and gentle wisdom, prepared to unravel another thread in the tapestry of the Guru's teachings. Mythili, her eyes bright with curiosity, and Pavan, his expression thoughtful, settled into their familiar places, ready to delve into the intricate relationship between the employer and the worker.

"Today," Professor began, his voice a calm current, "we explore a crucial aspect of the Guru's philosophy: The essential reciprocity between employer and worker. He understood that the success of any enterprise, indeed the very fabric of society, depends on the harmonious interaction between these two vital forces."

He introduced the chapter with a story, "Consider an incident recounted by A.D. Harisharma, a respected writer in the Malayalam Language. The Guru was resting at the Moothakunnam temple when two men,

Govindan and Shankaran, approached the Guru seeking counsel. They were locked in a dispute over wages."

"Shankaran, the worker, felt he was being underpaid by Govindan, his employer. Govindan, on the other hand, argued he was following the Guru's teachings of 'attain wealth through industry' and was providing employment. He claimed the wages were in line with local customs but acknowledged Shankaran's dissatisfaction."

Mythili, her brow furrowed, asked, "How did the Guru resolve this conflict?"

Professor's eyes twinkled. "The Guru, with his characteristic wisdom, used a simple analogy. He asked them if they had seen a bullock cart pulled by twin bullocks. 'Is it enough for the cart to move forward if the bullocks are strong?' he asked. 'No,' he replied, *If both the bullocks do not pull with one mind, will the cart move forward?"*

He likened their relationship to the bullocks. "The work that one of you does and the other does is like a moving bullock cart. Imagine that you are two bullocks who have to pull the cart. If both of you do not move forward with mutual interest, the cart will not move forward."

Pavan, intrigued, asked, "What was the Guru's message?"

"The Guru emphasized the interdependence of employer and worker. 'Govindan has invested the money. Will you get income if you put the money in a box and lock it?' the Guru asked. ' The work can only be done with the help of experienced people. Govindan gets income because of the support and services of experienced people like Shankaran. Is it right for Govindan not to remember this?"

He also acknowledged Shankaran's contribution. 'Does Shankaran have the money to do this work? No. Wasn't it because Govindan invested the money that Shankaran got the job? Shankaran himself admits that he has been living from this work for the past two or three years. Tomorrow, if Govindan refuses, won't Shankaran have to suffer, at least temporarily? Both parties should understand this and work together. God will bring you good.'

Mythili nodded thoughtfully. "The Guru's message is clear: mutual respect and understanding are essential for a healthy working relationship."

"Precisely," Professor affirmed. "This incident, though from a century ago, remains profoundly relevant today. It reinforces the fundamental truth that the success of any endeavor depends on the cooperation and mutual benefit of those involved."

He then expanded on the Guru's broader vision. "The Guru also highlighted the importance of an organization. 'A society cannot progress except through organization,' he said. 'If people come together and communicate with each other, they will naturally come closer. However, the purpose of organization should not be to create a community by bringing together only a particular class of people. The work of the organization should be intelligent, because it is the forerunner of future progress."

"These words were taken to heart by P.K. Bava , also known as Vadapuram Bava, in Alappuzha. Bava, from an economically privileged background, worked as a supervisor in a British-owned coir factory. He was known for his compassionate treatment of workers, a stark contrast to the prevailing practices of the time."

"The management demanded that Bava physically punish a worker named Muhammadali for alleged negligence. Bava, a staunch believer in the Guru's teachings, refused. He treated all workers with equality, compassion, and love. This refusal led to the tragic death of Muhammadali at the hands of goons hired by the management."

Pavan, his expression grim, asked, "What happened next?"

"Bava, deeply disturbed by this injustice, filed a case in the Alappuzha First Class Magistrate Court. However, the court dismissed the case, citing the workers' lack of education as a reason to discredit their testimony."

Mythili's eyes widened in disbelief. "That's appalling! How could the court disregard the workers' testimony simply because they were uneducated?"

"It was a reflection of the prevailing social attitudes of the time," Professor explained. "Bava, deeply saddened by this injustice, sought the Guru's counsel. He informed the Guru about the harsh working conditions, the long hours, and the inadequate wages faced by the workers."

"The Guru listened patiently and then offered a solution: 'Then form a group of job seekers. Let the workers be strong and independent under the power of the group."

"This advice led to the formation of the Travancore Labor Association, the first registered labor union in Kerala. It was a decisive moment in the history of labor rights in the region."

Pavan, his interest piqued, asked, "How did the Guru develop such a deep understanding of labor issues?"

"The Guru's understanding was profound and multifaceted," Professor replied. "He had a keen awareness of the global labor movements of the late 19th and early 20th centuries. His disciple, K. Ayyappan, through his monthly 'Sahodaran,' regularly published articles on Marxism, socialism, and the Russian Revolution. This exposure to global labor movements undoubtedly shaped the Guru's thinking."

"To truly grasp the significance of the Guru's advice, we need to understand the historical context of the global labor movement," Professor continued. "The late 19th century witnessed a surge in labor activism, driven by the harsh working conditions and exploitation faced by the workers in industrialized nations."

"One pivotal event was the May 1, 1866, protest in Chicago, USA, where workers demanded an eight-hour workday. This protest, though initially met with violence, ultimately led to the establishment of May 1st as International Workers' Day."

He then narrated the events of the Haymarket Square incident, : "On May 4th, a peaceful meeting in Haymarket Square turned violent when a bomb exploded, killing several police officers. This led to a crackdown on labor activists, but it also solidified May 1st as a symbol of workers' struggle."

"The International Socialist Conference in 1889 officially recognized May 1st as a day to commemorate the Haymarket martyrs and to advocate for workers' rights. This marked a turning point in the global labor movement."

Mythili, her eyes filled with empathy, asked, "What about the United States? How did they respond to May Day?"

"The United States, due to its political differences with communist countries during the Cold War, initially distanced itself from May Day celebrations," Professor explained. "However, under President Eisenhower, the US eventually recognized May Day as 'Loyalty Day,' while Labor Day is celebrated in September there."

"Despite the variations in how May Day is celebrated, the underlying principle of workers' rights has gained universal recognition," Professor continued. "Today, most countries acknowledge the importance of fair wages, reasonable working hours, and safe working conditions."

"The Guru's vision, however, went beyond the mere pursuit of economic rights. He sought to instill a sense of morality and social responsibility in the labor movement. He believed that workers' organizations should not only advocate for their members' rights but also contribute to the broader goals of peace, brotherhood, and equality."

Pavan, his analytical mind tussling with the complexities of the subject, asked, "How did the Guru reconcile his vision of worker empowerment with the need for social harmony?"

"The Guru understood that social harmony could only be achieved through justice and fairness," Professor replied. "He believed that workers' rights and social responsibility were not mutually exclusive. He saw them as two sides of the same coin, essential for building a just and prosperous society."

"He advocated for a system where employers and workers recognized their mutual dependence and worked together for the common windfall. He emphasized the importance of dialogue, negotiation, and compromise, promoting a culture of collaboration rather than confrontation."

"The Guru's vision," Professor concluded, "was not merely about creating a system of economic justice. It was about fostering a society where everyone, regardless of their social or economic status, felt valued and respected. He believed that true progress could only be achieved when everyone had the opportunity to contribute their talents and skills, and to share the fruits of their labor."

"His legacy challenges us to rethink the very nature of work and the relationship between employer and worker. It urges us to move beyond the narrow focus on economic efficiency and to embrace a broader vision of social justice and human dignity."

"The Guru's influence," Professor continued, his voice a steady stream of wisdom, "extended beyond the realm of labor unions. The Guru sought to transform the very relationship between employer and worker, fostering a sense of partnership and mutual respect. He envisioned a workplace where both parties recognized their interdependence and worked together towards a common goal."

He paused, allowing his words to resonate, then elaborated, " They challenged the traditional power dynamics of the workplace, advocating for a more egalitarian and collaborative environment. He believed that workers were not mere cogs in a machine but valuable contributors to the success of the enterprise. He emphasized the importance of recognizing their skills, respecting their dignity, and providing them with fair wages and decent working conditions."

Mythili, her expression thoughtful, asked, "Professor, how did the Guru's teachings address the potential for conflict between employers and workers? Did he offer specific guidelines for resolving disputes?"

Professor nodded, acknowledging the importance of her question. "That's a pivotal point, Mythili. The Guru recognized that conflict was an inevitable part of human interaction, including the relationship between employer and worker. However, he believed that conflict could be resolved peacefully and constructively through dialogue, negotiation, and compromise."

He then shared insights into the Guru's approach to conflict resolution. "The Guru reminded the importance of open communication, encouraging both employers and workers to express their concerns and to listen to each other's perspectives. He advocated for a spirit of empathy and understanding, urging both parties to see the situation from the other's point of view."

"He also stressed the importance of fairness and justice," Professor continued. "He believed that disputes should be resolved based on principles of equity and impartiality, ensuring that both parties were treated with respect and that their rights were protected."

Professor then delved into the practical implications of the Guru's teachings.

"The Guru's vision translated into concrete actions. He encouraged the formation of labor unions, empowering workers to collectively bargain for better wages and working conditions. He also urged employers to adopt more humane and ethical management practices, recognizing the value of the workforce and treating them with respect."

The Professor then shared examples of the Guru's direct involvement in resolving labor disputes. "There are numerous incidents where the Guru intervened in the conflicts between employers and workers, mediating disputes, and helping to find were mutually acceptable solutions . His interventions were always characterized by his wisdom, his compassion, and his unwavering commitment to justice."

"He often used simple analogies and stories to illustrate his points, making his teachings accessible to people from all walks of life. His ability to connect with people on a personal level, to understand their concerns, and to offer practical solutions was truly remarkable."

Pavan, his analytical mind seeking to understand the broader context, asked, "Professor, how did the Guru's vision align with the emerging labor movements of his time? Was he influenced by any specific ideologies or thinkers?"

The Professor paused, considering the complexity of the question. "The Guru's vision was undoubtedly influenced by the social and political currents of his time, including the rise of labor movements and socialist ideologies. However, his approach was unique, characterized by his emphasis on spirituality, morality, and social harmony."

Professor then elaborated on the influences that shaped the Guru's thinking. "He was deeply influenced by the ancient Indian philosophical tradition, which emphasized the interconnectedness of all beings and the importance of compassion and service. He also drew inspiration from the teachings of various religious and spiritual leaders, recognizing the common thread of humanism that ran through their messages."

"While he was aware of the Marxist analysis of class struggle, his approach was not based on confrontation or revolution. He sought to transform society through peaceful means, promoting dialogue, understanding, and cooperation. He believed that true progress could only be achieved through a change of heart, a transformation of individual consciousness."

Professor then returned to the narrative of P.K. Bava and the Travancore Labor Association, highlighting its significance in the history of labor rights in Kerala. "The Travancore Labor Association, formed under the Guru's guidance, was a pioneering organization. It not only fought for better wages and working conditions but also promoted education, social reform, and community development."

He then shared details about the association's activities and achievements. "The association organized peaceful protests and strikes, demanding fair treatment for workers. It also established schools and libraries, providing access to education for the children of workers. It played a vital role in raising awareness about social issues and in promoting a more just and equitable society."

"Its legacy continues to inspire labor activists and social reformers in Kerala and beyond," he continued. "It stands as a testament to the power of collective action and the enduring relevance of the Guru's vision."

Professor then expanded on the global context of labor movements, connecting the Guru's teachings to the broader struggle for workers' rights around the world. "The late 19th and early 20th centuries witnessed a surge in labor activism across the globe, driven by the harsh realities of industrialization and the exploitation of workers."

He then discussed key events in the history of the labor movement, including the May Day protests and the rise of socialist and communist ideologies. "These movements, while often characterized by conflict and confrontation, played a pivotal role in improving the lives of workers and in establishing basic labor rights."

"The Guru's vision, however, offered a unique perspective," he continued. "He sought to infuse the labor movement with a spirit of compassion and social responsibility, urging workers to not only fight for their own rights but also to contribute to the well-being of society as a whole."

Professor concluded the current discussions by reiterating the enduring relevance of the Guru's teachings on the relationship between employer and worker. "The Guru's vision offers a timeless message of harmony and cooperation. It reminds us that true progress can only be achieved when all members of society work together, respecting each other's rights and contributing their talents and skills to the common good."

"His legacy challenges us to build a world where work is not merely a means of earning a livelihood but also a source of dignity, fulfillment, and social connection. It calls upon us to create workplaces that are characterized by fairness, justice, and mutual respect, where both employers and workers can thrive and contribute to a more just and prosperous society."

Key Learnings from the discussions on the labor movement were condensed by Pavan as:

- **Mutual Interdependence:** The success of an enterprise relies on the mutual interest and cooperation between employers and employees. The Guru's analogy of the bullock cart emphasizes this interdependence.
- **Importance of Organization:** The Guru advocated for workers to organize, forming groups and unions to strengthen their position and advocate for their rights.

- **Fair Wages and Working Conditions:** The Guru stressed the importance of fair wages, reasonable working hours, and the elimination of exploitation.
- **Social Responsibility:** Beyond economic demands, the Guru envisioned labor organizations contributing to broader social goals like peace, brotherhood, and equality.
- **Global Labor Movements:** The text highlights the historical context of global labor movements, including the struggle for the eight-hour workday and the establishment of May Day.
- **Resolution through Dialogue:** The Guru's method of resolving conflict involved communication and understanding between the parties involved.

❖ ❖ ❖

18

A Model for Labor: Organizing for Equity and Dignity

The bustling cafeteria, a microcosm of society, provided an apt setting for Professor Shiva's lesson. The clatter of cutlery, the murmur of conversations, and the aroma of freshly brewed coffee formed a backdrop to the intellectual feast about to unfold. Mythili, her eyes sparkling with anticipation, and Pavan, his expression a blend of curiosity and contemplation, joined Professor at a corner table, their notebooks open and ready.

"Today," Professor began, his voice cutting through the ambient noise, "we delve into the Guru's unique model of labor organization, a model that transcended the conventional paradigms of his time and continues to hold relevance in the Indian complex economic landscape."

He gestured towards the lively scene around them. "Look around you. This cafeteria, like any workplace, is a symphony of diverse roles and responsibilities. From the cook to the cashier, everyone contributes bestows to the smooth functioning of this space. The Guru understood that the success of any enterprise, be it a small eatery or a large corporation, depends on the harmonious collaboration of all its stakeholders."

Pavan, ever the sensible, asked, "Professor, how did the Guru's model differ from the prevailing labor ideologies of his time? Wasn't the Industrial Revolution marked by intense class conflict?"

"Indeed," Professor asserted, his eyes reflecting the historical complexities. "The Industrial Revolution, with its unprecedented technological advancements, brought about a dramatic shift in the production sector. While it led to increased productivity and economic growth, it also created a stark divide between the capitalist class and the working class. The relentless pursuit of profit maximization often resulted in the exploitation of workers, leading to widespread discontent and social unrest."

He paused, allowing his words to sink in, then elaborated, "The Guru, like Karl Marx, recognized the inherent injustice of exploitation. However, he offered a fundamentally different approach to addressing this issue. While Marx advocated for class struggle and the dictatorship of the proletariat, the Guru emphasized the importance of moral transformation and social harmony."

Mythili, her brow furrowed in thought, asked, "So, the Guru believed in a more collaborative approach, rather than a confrontational one?"

"Precisely," Professor confirmed. "He believed that true and lasting change could only be achieved through a transformation of consciousness, a shift from 'distorted intelligence' to 'righteous intelligence.' He emphasized the importance of cultivating empathy, compassion, and a sense of shared responsibility among both employers and workers."

He then delved into the specific context of India during the Guru's time. "It's important to remember that India's social landscape was significantly different from that of Europe. While Europe was grappling with class conflict, India was burdened by the oppressive caste system. The Guru understood that any attempt to address labor issues in India had to take into account the complex interplay of class and caste."

"He recognized that the caste system, with its inherent hierarchy and discrimination, had deeply influenced the class structure, creating a unique form of exploitation that went beyond mere economic disparities. He understood that true liberation required not only the dismantling of class barriers but also the eradication of caste-based discrimination."

Pavan, his interest piqued, asked, "How did the Guru's model address the issue of individual freedom?"

"The Guru was a devoted advocate of individual freedom," Professor replied. "He understood that true liberation encompassed both economic and political freedom. He welcomed the advent of democratic governance in India, recognizing it as a crucial step towards empowering individuals and safeguarding their rights."

He then contrasted the Guru's approach with that of Marx and Engels. "While Marx and Engels believed in the necessity of a 'dictatorship of the proletariat' to achieve democracy, the Guru emphasized the importance of upholding the rule of law and respecting individual liberties. He believed that true democracy could only be achieved through peaceful and non-violent means."

"He understood that India, with its diverse cultural and religious traditions, required a model of social transformation that was rooted in its own unique context. He believed that morality and spirituality played a key role in shaping individual behavior and promoting social harmony."

The Professor then shifted the focus to the historical context of the Indian labor movement. "The father of the Indian labor movement, N.M. Lokhande was inspired by Mahatma Jyoti Rao Phule, a leader of the social reform movement in Maharashtra. Lokhande's efforts to organize workers and form trade unions laid the foundation for the modern labor movement in India."

Professor then highlighted the significance of the Madras Labor Union, formed in 1918. "The Madras Labor Union, which organized the first May Day celebration in India in 1923, played a pivotal role in popularizing the concept of workers' rights and solidarity."

"In Kerala, the labor movement was spearheaded by P.K. Bava, who was inspired by the Guru's teachings," Professor continued. "Bava, also known as Vadapuram Bava, played a crucial role in organizing workers and forming the Travancore Labor Association, the first registered labor union in Kerala."

He then delved into the historical context of labor struggles in Kerala. "Kerala has a rich history of labor activism, dating back to the 19th century. The farmers' strike led by Arattupuzha Velayudapanikar in 1866, which coincided with the workers' protests in Chicago, is considered to be one of the earliest farmers' strikes in the world."

"Mahatma Ayyankali, another prominent social reformer, also led numerous farmers' strikes, advocating for the rights of marginalized communities. His close association with the Guru undoubtedly shaped his approach to social activism."

"T.K. Madhavan, a disciple of the Guru, led the farmers' strike in Kuttanad during 1915-20, further demonstrating the strong connection between the Guru's teachings and the labor movement in Kerala."

Professor then recounted the incident at Harrison's Company in 1915 at Kollam, where workers protested against harsh working conditions. "The Guru, who was at Kollam then, deeply disturbed by the plight of the workers, closely monitored the situation. He recognized the need for organized labor to address the harsh exploitation faced by workers."

He then highlighted the Guru's advice to Sahodaran Ayyappan, urging him to focus on the upliftment of workers. "Ayyappan, following the Guru's guidance, published articles in his periodicals 'Sahodaran' and 'Velakkaran,' raising awareness about the plight of workers and advocating for their rights."

"He also formed labor organizations, such as the *'Vypin Thozhilali Sangam'* and the 'Ochamthuruth Thozhilali Union,' although these organizations faced challenges due to the workers' fear of revenge from employers."

The Professor then returned to the story of P.K. Bava and the Travancore Labor Association. "Bava, inspired by the Guru's motto, 'Form a group of workers, let them be strong and independent in the strength of the group,' took the lead in forming the Travancore Labor Association in 1922."

He then highlighted the significance of the association's formation. "The Travancore Labor Association's formation was a landmark event in the history of the Indian labor movement, particularly because it predated the enactment of the Trade Union Act in 1926."

"The association's leadership included prominent individuals from diverse backgrounds, such as M.K. Antony, P.C. Muhammad, Kesari Balakrishna Pillai, and P. Keshavadev, demonstrating its inclusive and non-sectarian character."

The Professor then addressed the attempts by certain historians to downplay the significance of the Travancore Labor Association. "Unfortunately, some historians, influenced by caste biases, have attempted to belittle the association's contributions, falsely claiming that it was a 'single caste organization.' This is a deliberate attempt to distort history and undermine the association's legacy."

He then emphasized the crucial role played by Swami Satyavrata, the Guru's monk disciple, in the association's formation. "Swami Satyavrata, representative of the Guru, conveyed the Guru's message to the workers at the inaugural meeting of the association. The Guru's message, 'The time for workers to be afraid is coming, so go forward with courage and gain the trust of everyone,' served as a guiding principle for the association's activities."

"The Guru also sent a one-rupee coin to P.K. Bava, symbolizing his support and blessings for the association's work."

Professor then highlighted the unique blend of ideologies that characterized the Travancore Labor Association. "The association's office displayed pictures of both Sree Narayana Guru and Karl Marx, reflecting Bava's commitment to achieving both social equality and ethical labor practices."

"Bava's leadership style was characterized by his focus on building organizational strength, fostering a sense of brotherhood among workers, and promoting social reform. He organized medical camps, promoted literacy, and advocated for abstinence from alcohol."

He then discussed the publication 'Thozhilali', which was started under Bava's editorship. "It served as a platform for disseminating information about the workers' rights and for promoting social awareness." 'Thozhilali' in the local language denotes 'worker' in English.

Professor then summarized the Guru's vision for labor organization, drawing from his writings and the articles published in 'Sahodaran' and 'Velakkaran.' "The Guru's vision encompassed several key principles:

- Workers should organize themselves and become strong regardless of caste, religion, gender, and class, abandoning superstitions and senseless rituals.
- In the workplace, create and maintain compassion, love, friendship, brotherhood, simplicity, sacrifice, and complete identification between worker and employer.
- Recognize that spiritual progress shapes intellectual development and morality, and dialogue among workers is essential.
- Promote goodwill, not hatred; seek understanding, not victory through argument.
- Guide colleagues towards life, not death.
- Utilize organizational power to eradicate social, economic, intellectual, and spiritual inequality caused by caste and religious ideologies.
- Understand that both the investors and workers are necessary, fostering mutual interest in the workplace.
- Recognize that the distinction between employer and worker should not lead to the elimination of either, as such thinking is irrational.

"Let us also consider the perspective of Lenin," Professor continued, "who led the government in the Soviet Union based on Marxist philosophy. Lenin stated, 'Morality consists in a conscious, disciplined, and joint mass struggle against the exploiters. We do not believe in eternal morality. We expose all the myths about morality. That is morality, which helps to destroy the exploitative society and to organize all the working people around the working class and create a communist society."

"While Lenin focused on class struggle as the means to achieve a just society, the Guru emphasized the importance of morality and spirituality in transforming both individuals and society," the Professor explained. "He believed that true and lasting change could only be achieved through a holistic approach that addressed both the material and the spiritual needs of humanity."

"The Guru's vision," Professor concluded, his voice resonating with conviction, "provides a timeless and enduring model for labor organization, one that is particularly relevant in a democratic society like India. He showed us that it is possible to protect the rights of workers while also upholding moral principles and fostering social harmony. His legacy challenges us to build a world where work is not merely a means of survival but a source of dignity, fulfillment, and social connection. Let us follow the path shown by this great Guru."

Key Learnings from the current discussion were condensed by the Professor as:

- ***Beyond Class Struggle:*** *The Guru's labor organization model differed from Marxist ideologies by emphasizing moral transformation and social harmony over class struggle. He advocated for a shift from "distorted intelligence" to "righteous intelligence."*
- ***Addressing Caste and Class:*** *The Guru recognized the unique Indian context, where the caste system significantly influenced class structures. He believed true liberation required addressing both caste-based discrimination and class exploitation.*
- ***Importance of Individual Freedom:*** *The Guru supported democratic governance and individual liberties, advocating for peaceful means of social transformation and rejecting the concept of a "dictatorship of the proletariat."*
- ***Holistic Worker Empowerment:*** *The Guru's vision extended beyond economic rights, promoting spiritual and intellectual development. He emphasized building workplaces characterized by compassion, brotherhood, and mutual respect.*
- ***Moral and Ethical Labor Practices:*** *The Guru stressed the importance of morality and ethical conduct in labor organizations, advocating for dialogue, understanding, and cooperation between employers and workers, and that the workforce should be organized regardless of caste, creed, or gender.*

19

SUSTAINABILITY AND PROSPERITY: CLEANLINESS AND NATURE CONSERVATION

The beach, a vast expanse of golden sand caressed by the rhythmic dance of the waves, served as a serene lecture hall. Professor, his eyes reflecting the boundless horizon, prepared to unveil another facet of the Guru's profound wisdom. Mythili, her notebook open, and Pavan, his expression thoughtful, joined him on a cluster of sun-warmed rocks, ready to absorb the lessons carried on the gentle sea breeze.

"Today," Professor began, his voice a soothing melody against the backdrop of the ocean's murmur, "we will explore the Guru's unwavering commitment to cleanliness and nature conservation, two pillars of his philosophy that have gained renewed significance in the increasingly fragile world."

He gestured towards the vast breadth of the sea. "The recent global pandemic has served as a stark reminder of the interconnectedness of human health and environmental well-being. The Guru, with his characteristic foresight, recognized this connection long ago, advocating for practices that would ensure both individual and collective well-being."

Pavan, his gaze fixed on the distant horizon, asked, "Professor, what led the Guru to emphasize cleanliness and nature conservation so strongly?"

"The Guru understood that true progress encompassed not only economic and social development but also the cultivation of healthy habits and a harmonious relationship with nature," Professor replied. "He recognized that cleanliness was not merely a matter of hygiene but a fundamental aspect of personal and societal well-being."

He then recounted the Guru's early teachings on cleanliness. "Even before the establishment of the Sivagiri pilgrimage, the Guru emphasized the importance of cleanliness. In 1886, at Aruvippuram, he advised devotees to maintain personal hygiene, including daily bathing, clean clothing, and wholesome food. He insisted, 'If there is cleanliness in the body, then there will be cleanliness in the food and the house.'"

Mythili, her brow furrowed in thought, asked, "How did the Guru's emphasis on cleanliness relate to the social issues of his time?"

"The Guru used cleanliness as a tool for social reform," Professor explained. "In a society plagued by untouchability and caste discrimination, he supported universal cleanliness, proclaiming that if everyone practiced hygiene, social barriers would naturally dissolve. He urged, 'Everyone should strictly follow cleanliness, untouchability will change itself, and there should be no fuss.'"

He then elaborated on the Guru's comprehensive approach to cleanliness. "The Guru expanded the concept of cleanliness beyond mere physical hygiene. He advocated for the practice of 'five cleanliness's' : cleanliness of body, speech, mind, senses, and home. He believed that true purity encompassed all aspects of human existence."

"He emphasized the importance of speaking truthfully and kindly, cultivating a pure mind free from hatred and jealousy, exercising restraint over the senses, and maintaining a clean and orderly home," Professor continued. "He saw cleanliness as a pathway to both physical and spiritual well-being."

"The Guru also stressed the importance of abstaining from alcohol," Professor added. "He recognized the devastating impact of alcohol on individuals and families, and he urged his followers to adopt a life of sobriety. He famously declared, "Alcohol is poison, do not make it, do not sell it, do not give it, do not drink it."

He then shared statistics illustrating the impact of the Guru's teachings on alcohol abstinence. "Government statistics reveal the profound influence of the Guru's teachings. In 1901, 10 percent of the Ezhava population was employed in the toddy plantation sector. By 1931, this number had dropped to four percent, demonstrating the significant shift in behavior."

Pavan, his interest piqued, asked, "What is the connection between cleanliness and economic philosophy, Professor?"

"Cleanliness is intrinsically linked to economic well-being," Professor replied. "A healthy workforce is a productive workforce. The Guru understood that maintaining cleanliness was essential for improving the health, knowledge, and lifestyle of individuals, thereby contributing to the overall economic prosperity of the society."

"Furthermore, ethical conduct is crucial for sustainable economic activity," Professor continued. "The Guru's teachings on cleanliness and morality reinforced the importance of ethical behavior in all aspects of life, including economic endeavors. He emphasized the principle that 'Dharma is the supreme God,' advocating for ethical conduct in all spheres of life."

Professor then shifted the focus to the Guru's profound insights on nature conservation. "The Guru was a pioneer in championing for nature conservation in Kerala," he said. "Long before the rise of environmental movements, he recognized the delicate balance between human activity and the natural world."

He quoted the Guru's powerful words on the destructive impact of human greed. The Guru observed, 'No other animal has untiring needs except humans. They are on a rampage of destruction all over the world. They spread a black shadow of emptiness wherever they go; they cut down and destroy all the trees. They devastate the green nature. Instead, they build dirty, smoky cities. All this is necessary for their unbridled world. They are not satisfied with the earth alone. They dig deep into the earth and break the bonds of this sphere. Man, who prides himself on being more intelligent than other animals, does not know what he is doing to himself. Oh! This man will destroy everything, and that is why he is satisfied. If the tragic consequences of his actions had only affected the human race, it would have been no problem. Don't they also deprive other living beings of their freedom?"

Mythili, her eyes filled with concern, asked, "How relevant are these words in today's world, Professor?"

"The Guru's words are more relevant than ever," Professor replied. "Our planet is facing unprecedented environmental challenges, including deforestation, climate change, and pollution. The Guru's warnings about the destructive impact of human greed have become a stark reality."

The Guru's call for nature conservation aligns with his economic vision of sustainable prosperity. By advocating for responsible resource use, he anticipated modern concepts like circular economies, where environmental stewardship supports long-term economic stability.

"The Guru emphasized the interconnectedness of humans and nature," Professor continued. "He stressed the importance of living in harmony with the natural world, recognizing that human well-being is inextricably linked to the health of the planet."

He then shared the Guru's insights from the 'Atmopadesa Satakam'. "In his well acclaimed work, Atmapadesa *Satakam* (Verse 43), the Guru wrote, 'Nature is like a whirlwind, even good deeds are whirling,' symbolizing the dynamic interplay between human actions and the environment. This reflects his belief that economic activities must respect natural limits. He emphasized that humans should live on this earth subject to the laws of nature."

"The Guru understood that nature has the power to shape human destiny," Professor explained. "He recognized that even the most powerful individuals and societies are subject to the forces of nature. He urged humans to respect and protect the natural world, recognizing its inherent value."

Professor then shared the inspiring story of T.N. Seshan, former Chief Election Commissioner of India, to illustrate the importance of empathy and compassion towards nature. "Seshan, during a car journey, witnessed a young boy refusing to give away sparrow nests, despite being offered a reward. The boy explained that he couldn't bear to see the mother sparrow cry for her lost chicks."

"This incident deeply moved Seshan, who realized that true humanity lies not in accumulating wealth or knowledge but in cultivating empathy and compassion towards all living beings," Professor concluded. "As Seshan himself stated, Knowledge means knowing nature. We do not understand anything by accumulating a lot of information. What makes life happy is knowledge, consciousness, love, compassion, and understanding. Human life that forgets nature will not bring eternal peace."

"The Guru taught us the same lesson a century ago," Professor emphasized. "He urged us to live in harmony with nature, to respect all living beings, and to cultivate a life of simplicity and compassion. Let us heed his wisdom and strive to build a world where cleanliness and nature conservation are not mere ideals but a way of life."

Key Learnings from the current discussion were summarized by the Professor as:

- ***Cleanliness as a Foundation:*** *The Guru viewed cleanliness as essential for personal and societal well-being, encompassing physical hygiene, purity of speech and mind, and a clean environment.*
- ***Social Reform through Hygiene:*** *The Guru advocated for universal cleanliness as a means to dismantle social barriers, believing that it could transcend caste and discrimination.*
- ***Cleanliness:*** *The Guru featured the practice of cleanliness of body, speech, mind, senses, and home, for holistic purity.*
- ***Abstinence from Alcohol:*** *The Guru strongly condemned alcohol consumption, recognizing that it has detrimental effects on individuals and families.*
- ***Nature Conservation:*** *The Guru was a pioneer in advocating for nature conservation, recognizing the interconnectedness of humans and the environment.*
- ***Warning against Greed:*** *The Guru cautioned against the destructive impact of human greed on the natural world, emphasizing the need for sustainable practices.*
- ***Harmony with Nature:*** *The Guru stressed the importance of living in harmony with nature, recognizing its power and the need for human respect and protection.*
- ***Empathy and Compassion:*** *The story of T.N. Seshan highlights the importance of empathy and compassion towards all living beings, reflecting the Guru's teachings.*

20

Prudence and Progress: Avoiding Complacency on the Path to Success

Professor Siva's chamber, a sanctuary of intellectual pursuit, hummed with a quiet energy. The bookshelves, laden with volumes spanning centuries, stood as silent witnesses to countless hours of contemplation. The scent of old paper and sandalwood incense drifted in the air, creating an atmosphere that invited deep thought. Mythili and Pavan, notebooks in hand, settled into the comfortable chairs, their minds ready to absorb the wisdom Professor was about to share.

"Welcome back," Professor said, his voice a warm, reassuring tone. "Today, we will delve deeper into the Guru's profound teachings on economy and the avoidance of waste. These principles, far from being outdated, are more relevant than ever in our modern, consumer-driven world."

Mythili, her pen poised over her notebook, asked, "the Professor, we know the Guru championed simplicity. But how did he specifically address the concept of 'waste' in a broader economic context?"

"The Guru understood that waste wasn't just about throwing things away," Professor explained. "It was about the misuse of resources, whether time, money, or natural assets. He saw waste as a form of spiritual and economic depletion. Traditional financial management often tolerated a certain level of waste, accepting it as a necessary evil. The Guru, however, insisted that waste could and should be eliminated."

Professor paused, allowing his words to sink in, then continued, "To truly appreciate his perspective, we need to understand how he categorized wealth. He recognized personal, corporate, and public wealth, and he believed that the principles of frugality applied to all three. Think of it like a farm: if you waste seeds, water, or fertile soil in your personal plot, your family suffers. If a corporation wastes resources, it affects the employees and shareholders. And if a government wastes public funds, the entire nation senses the impact."

Pavan, his brow furrowed in thought, asked, "But how did the Guru demonstrate this in his own life? It's easy to discourse about simplicity, but it's another thing to live it."

"Ah, that's where The Guru's example becomes so powerful," Professor responded, his eyes gleaming with admiration. "His life was a living testament to his teachings. Dharmananda Swami, his lifelong companion, described the guru as a man of great physical beauty and inner light, dressed in simple white cloth, devoid of any ornamentation. He didn't engage in elaborate rituals or accumulate material possessions. He lived a life of complete detachment."

Professor shared a story: "Once, a wealthy devotee offered The Guru a silk shawl embroidered with gold thread. The Guru politely declined, saying, 'My body is content with simple cotton. This shawl would only burden me.' He then suggested the devotee donate the shawl to a poor family who needed warm clothing. This wasn't just about personal frugality; it was about diverting resources to where they were truly needed."

Professor then quoted Nataraja Guru, emphasizing the significance of the Guru's simple attire as "decisive for economic prosperity." "The Guru deduced that true wealth wasn't about outward appearances or material possessions. It was about inner contentment and spiritual fulfillment. He also emphasized the importance of ethical wealth acquisition. He encouraged individuals to earn their livelihood through honest means, such as agriculture, trade, and handicrafts."

Professor shared another anecdote: "A group of merchants once sought the Guru's blessing for their business. They told him they were making substantial profits, but they were also engaging in some unethical practices to maximize their gains. The Guru listened patiently, then said, 'True prosperity comes from honest labor. If your wealth is built on dishonesty or fraud, it will crumble like sand.' He urged them to conduct their business ethically, even if it meant sacrificing some profit."

Mythili asked, "What about his views on temples and religious ceremonies? Weren't those often extravagant?"

"The Guru was a radical reformer in that regard," Professor said with a smile. "He advocated for simplicity and practicality in temple construction and religious practices. He urged people to build clean and functional temples, focusing on spiritual enlightenment rather than intricate rituals and extravagant displays. He advised, 'Temples do not need to be built in the old style by spending a lot of money.' He believed that temples should be centers of learning and social service, not just places of worship."

Professor shared an example: "When a group of devotees planned to build a grand temple with ornate carvings and gold-plated domes, the Guru advised them to build a simple structure with a spacious hall for lectures and discussions. He suggested they use the remaining funds to establish a school and a library for the community. The Guru added, 'True worship is serving humanity. A school and a library will illuminate the minds of the people, which is the greatest offering you can make."

"The Guru also challenged the prevailing social customs of his time," Professor continued. "He strongly protested the habit of spending money on unnecessary and unscientific rituals, such as elaborate marriage ceremonies, *Tirandukuli*, *Pulikudi*, and post-death rituals. These ceremonies often pushed families into crippling debt. He saw them as a form of social and economic exploitation."

Professor then shared the impact of the Guru's teachings: "His call to end these unethical practices had a profound impact on the society. Many families were saved from falling into debt traps, and a more rational and practical approach to social customs began to emerge. Consider the *Tirandukuli* ceremony, which involved lavish feasts and gifts when a girl reached puberty. The Guru pointed out that this ceremony often led to families selling their land or borrowing money at exorbitant interest rates. He said, 'True celebration is about the girl's well-being, not about extravagant displays.' He suggested simple, meaningful rituals that didn't burden the family financially."

Pavan asked, "How did he address post-death ceremonies, which are often very elaborate in Indian culture?"

"The Guru advocated for simplicity and practicality in post-death ceremonies," Professor replied. "He urged people to avoid extravagant displays of grief and instead focus on prayers and charitable acts in memory of the deceased. He suggested that donating money to religious institutions in the name of the deceased would be more beneficial than spending it on elaborate rituals."

He shared a story: "Once, a better-off man planned to hold a grand feast on the anniversary of his father's death, inviting hundreds of people and spending a fortune. The Guru visited him and said, 'Your father would have wanted you to help those in need, not to waste money on a lavish feast. Donate the money to a school or a hospital in his name. That would be a true tribute to his memory.' The man was deeply moved and followed the Guru's advice."

"The Guru also provided clear guidelines for conducting simple and meaningful marriage ceremonies," Professor continued. "He specialized in small and intimate weddings, focusing on the spiritual union of the couple rather than extravagant displays of wealth. He suggested that parents deposit the money they intended to spend on the wedding into a savings account and gift it to their children."

Professor shared a personal story: "My own grandfather, inspired by the Guru's teachings, had a simple wedding with only close family and friends. He used the money he saved to buy a small plot of land, which eventually became our family home. This act of frugality and foresight laid the foundation for our family's prosperity."

Mythili asked, "What about the matriarchal nephew system? That was a major social issue at the time."

"The Guru recognized the inherent inequality in the nephew system," Professor replied. "He advocated for a law that would ensure that the wife and children would inherit a man's wealth, thereby protecting their financial security. He saw this as a matter of justice and fairness."

Professor then shared C.V. Kunjuraman's assessment of the economic impact of The Guru's reforms. "Kunjuraman estimated that the Guru's reforms had saved the Ezhava community crores of rupees. This demonstrates the profound economic impact of The Guru's teachings. It was not just about changing customs; it was about transforming the economic landscape of the community."

"The Guru also waged a relentless campaign against alcoholism," Professor added. "He recognized the devastating impact of alcohol on individuals, families, and society. He urged people to abstain from alcohol and promoted alternative livelihoods for those involved in the production and sale of alcohol."

He shared a powerful story: "The Guru once visited a village where many men were addicted to toddy. He went from house to house, talking to the heads and their families, explaining the harmful effects of alcohol. He then organized a meeting and urged the village elders to close the toddy shops. He said, 'Your children are starving, your wives are suffering, and your homes are falling apart because of this poisonous item. Close the liquor shops and use your energy to build a better future.' His words had a profound impact, and the village eventually became alcohol-free."

The Professor shared a touching story: "A poor woman once came to the Guru, seeking his blessing for her daughter's marriage. She had very little money and was worried about how she would afford the wedding. The Guru listened to her patiently, then said, 'Don't worry. A simple ceremony with the blessings of your family and friends is more valuable than any extravagant display. Use the money you have to secure your daughter's future, not to impress others.' He then gave her a small amount of money from his own meager possessions, saying, 'This is my blessing. Use it wisely.' The woman was deeply touched by the Guru's compassion and followed his advice, holding a simple but meaningful wedding for her daughter." Based on this incident, the Guru issued a press note insisting that all his devotees go for simple marriage functions, specifying the total number of participants as ten. This was published in 'Kerala Kaumudi', a widely circulated newspaper edited by C.V. Kunjuraman. It was also a news item in Vivokodayam, edited by Mahakavi Kumaran Asan. This news was well appreciated by the readers, and they started practicing the advice of the Guru.

"The Guru also provided clear instructions for cutting costs in *Ishwara Puja* and *Homa*," Professor added. "He demonstrated the power of simple and meaningful rituals, composing his own *Homa Mantra* and urging his followers to perform *Homa* at the lowest cost. He believed that the essence of worship lay in devotion and sincerity, not in elaborate rituals or expensive offerings."

The Professor then recited the Guru's *Homa Mantra*, explaining its meaning and significance. "This mantra, composed by the Guru, exemplifies his emphasis on simplicity and practicality in religious practices. It focuses on the inner fire of knowledge and devotion, rather than external rituals."

The Professor then transitioned to the relevance of the Guru's teachings to modern life, particularly in the realm of public finance. "The Guru's teachings are more relevant than ever," Professor replied. "In an era of rampant consumerism and environmental degradation, his emphasis on mindful consumption and responsible resource utilization is crucial for building a sustainable future. His ideas extend beyond personal and corporate finance and are profoundly applicable to government spending."

The Professor emphasized the importance of ethical economic practices. "The Guru believed that economic activity should be guided by ethical principles. He condemned corruption, exploitation, and greed, and he urged individuals and businesses to act with integrity and compassion. He said, Wealth acquired through unethical means is like a poisoned well; it may quench your thirst for a while, but it will eventually lead to ruin."

The Professor shared a powerful example: "A wealthy businessman, known for his ruthless business practices, once sought the Guru's advice. The Guru listened to him, then said, 'Your wealth is built on the suffering of others. True prosperity comes from serving humanity, not exploiting it. Change your ways and use your wealth to help those in need.' The businessman was deeply affected by the Guru's words and transformed his business practices, becoming a philanthropist and a force for good in the community."

The Professor then discussed the application of the Guru's teachings to public finance management. "The Guru's principles of frugality and avoidance of waste are equally applicable to government spending. He urged governments to eliminate wasteful expenditures and prioritize investments that benefit society. He would have been a strong advocate for transparent budgeting and accountable governance."

"The Guru's emphasis on frugality in personal and community contexts suggests he would advocate for efficient public spending. His support for transparent institutions like the SNDP Yogam implies a belief in accountable resource management, a principle reflected in modern budgeting practices, specifically Zero-Base Budgeting. He would have been appalled by corruption and the misuse of public funds."

He provided a modern analogy: "Imagine a government project to build a new road. The Guru would have insisted on a thorough cost-benefit analysis, ensuring that the project was truly necessary and that the funds were used efficiently. He would have condemned any form of corruption or wasteful spending, ensuring that the project served the public good, not the interests of a few."

"The Guru's teachings on frugality and avoidance of waste provide a timeless and enduring framework for economic prosperity," Professor concluded, his voice resonating with conviction. "He showed us that true wealth lies not in material possessions but in mindful consumption, responsible resource utilization, and ethical conduct. His vision was not just about individual prosperity but about creating a just and sustainable society. Let us embrace his wisdom and strive to build a world where frugality and sustainability are the cornerstones of our economic practices, from our personal lives to the highest levels of this government."

He paused, allowing his words to settle in the minds of Mythili and Pavan, and then added, "Let us remember that frugality is not about deprivation; it is about making judicious choices. It is about valuing quality over quantity, about using resources wisely, and about prioritizing the needs of others over our own desires. It's about living a life of purpose and meaning, rather than being driven by the endless pursuit of material possessions. In a world obsessed with consumption, The Guru's teachings offer a refreshing and vital alternative – a path to true prosperity, both economic and spiritual."

Key Learnings from the current session were resumed by the Professor as:

- ***Frugality as a Core Principle:*** *The Guru punctuated frugality and the avoidance of waste in all aspects of life, encompassing personal, corporate, and public finances. He viewed waste as a misuse of resources and a form of spiritual and economic depletion.*
- ***Simplicity and Detachment:*** *The Guru's own life exemplified simplicity and detachment from material possessions. He believed that true wealth lay in spiritual fulfillment and ethical wealth acquisition, not in outward appearances or material accumulation.*
- ***Practicality in Religious Practices:*** *The Guru insisted on simplicity and practicality in temple construction and religious ceremonies, discouraging extravagant displays and prioritizing spiritual enlightenment and social service.*
- ***Reform of Social Customs:*** *The challenged wasteful social customs, such as elaborate marriage ceremonies and post-death rituals, promoting more rational and practical approaches that did not burden families financially.*
- ***Relevance to Modern Life:*** *The Guru's teachings on frugality and waste avoidance are highly relevant to modern life, particularly in addressing*

issues of consumerism, environmental degradation, and responsible public finance management. He highlighted ethical economic practices and the importance of using resources wisely for the benefit of society.

❖ ❖ ❖

21

Inspired by the Sage: Success Stories of the Guru's Disciples

The gentle breeze carried the scent of the sea, mingling with the fragrance of jasmine and plumeria that wafted from the nearby gardens. Professor, Mythili, and Pavan stood on the hallowed grounds of Sivagiri, Thiruvananthapuram, the Mahasamadhi place of the Great Guru. It requires special mention in this context that the Guru's birthplace, Chempazhanthi in Thiruvananthapuram, is located 30 kilometers away from the Sivagiri Hills.

Sivagiri is the place where the seeds of social and economic transformation were sown. The sun cast long shadows, painting the landscape in hues of gold and amber, as Professor began to weave a tale of entrepreneurship and empowerment.

"Here, in this humble village, a vision was born, a vision that transcended the limitations of caste and creed, embracing the boundless potential of humanity," Professor began, his voice resonating with the spirit of the place. "The Guru's message was clear: 'One caste, one religion, one God for humanity.' He understood that the true progress required not just spiritual awakening, but also the material upliftment of all, regardless of their social standing."

Professor gestured towards the simple beauty of the surroundings. "In his time, economic opportunities were often restricted by social barriers. But the Guru's vision extended beyond these limitations. He sought to create a society where everyone had access to education, resources, and the means to achieve economic independence."

Her eyes reflecting the historical significance of the place, Mythili asked, "Professor, how did the Guru inspire people to become entrepreneurs in a society where such opportunities were often denied?"

"The Guru's approach was both practical and profound," Professor explained. "He understood that entrepreneurship was not just about business acumen; it was about cultivating a mindset of self-reliance, innovation, and social responsibility. He provided guidance, instilled confidence, and offered unwavering support to those who dared to dream of a better future."

Pavan, ever eager to understand the mechanics of economic progress, enquired, "What were the key principles that guided the Guru's vision for economic empowerment?"

"The Guru underlined the importance of knowledge, organization, and industry as the pillars of economic prosperity," Professor replied. "The guru believed that education was the foundation for individual growth and societal progress. He encouraged people to acquire knowledge, to organize themselves into cooperatives and associations, and to engage in productive economic activities."

Professor paused, allowing the weight of the Guru's words to settle, then continued, "The Guru recognized the pivotal role of entrepreneurship in driving economic growth. He understood that individuals, partnerships, joint stock companies, and cooperatives were all essential components of a thriving economy. He also recognized that the traditional definition of 'industry' was expanding, encompassing not just manufacturing but also agriculture, commerce, and other services. He was a visionary, far ahead of his time."

The Professor then addressed the fundamental question of what constitutes an entrepreneur. "The Guru understood that an entrepreneur is more than just a businessman. He's a visionary, a risk-taker, a leader. He possesses the mental courage to create, manage, and develop a business. He is resilient in the face of uncertainty and capable of turning challenges into opportunities. He's not just driven by profit but also by a desire to contribute to the well-being of society."

He elaborated on the qualities that the Guru sought in entrepreneurs. "He looked for individuals with enthusiasm, dedication, leadership potential, and the ability to make sound decisions. He valued those who could identify and utilize resources effectively, who were not afraid to innovate, and who were committed to ethical business practices. He also understood that entrepreneurs were not just born; they were nurtured through education, training, and experience. He knew that in a rapidly evolving world, continuous learning and adaptation were essential for success."

"Now, let me share some inspiring stories of entrepreneurs who achieved remarkable success through the Guru's guidance and blessings," Professor elaborated, his eyes twinkling with anticipation. "These stories are not just about business acumen; they're about the transformative power of vision, perseverance, and social responsibility."

The Professor began with the story of C.R. Kesavan Vaidyan. "In 1926, a young man named Kesavan, burdened by debt and despair, came to the Guru seeking relief and direction. The Guru, recognizing Kesavan's potential, did not offer him charity; he offered him a vision. He told Kesavan to return home, settle his debts, and then pursue the study of Siddha Vaidya. He also gave him a silver coin, a symbol of his blessing and a reminder of his faith in Kesavan's abilities."

"Kesavan followed the Guru's advice," Professor continued. "He studied Siddha Vaidya, became a physician, and established his own practice. But his entrepreneurial spirit did not stop there. He developed an Ayurvedic toilet soap called 'Chandrika,' using a special formula he learned from the Guru's direct disciple, Ramananda Swami. Chandrika soap became a global sensation, exported to more than 85 countries, a testament to Kesavan's business acumen and the power of traditional knowledge."

"Kesavan Vaidyan never forgot The Guru's guidance," Professor intensified. "He used his wealth and influence to promote education, establish social service institutions, and even served as the President of the SNDP Yogam, carrying forward the Guru's vision of social upliftment."

"And then there's the story of Medimix soap," Professor added. "Dr. Sidhan, a descendant of Cholayil Kunjumami Vaidyan, who treated the Guru during his last days, developed Medimix soap using a special oil formulated by his ancestor. He was inspired by the global success of Chandrika soap and the Guru's emphasis on utilizing traditional knowledge for economic development. He saw in Chandrika's success a validation of the potential of Ayurvedic products in the global market."

"Another remarkable entrepreneur was M.P. Moothedath," Professor said. "M.P. Moothedath, a railway clerk, approached the Guru with a dream of becoming a railway contractor. The Guru, recognizing Moothedath's sharp intellect and dedication, encouraged him to pursue his ambition. He even advised him to seek financial support from the Cochin National Bank, established by Bodhananda Swami, demonstrating his understanding of the importance of access to capital for aspiring entrepreneurs."

"Moothedath went on to become a highly successful railway contractor," Professor continued. "He never forgot the Guru's kindness and support. He donated the Guru's idol and Samadhi Mandir to Sivagiri, a testament to his gratitude and his commitment to the Guru's vision. He also established the Makotha Memorial Trust, providing educational support to financially disadvantaged students, recognizing the transformative power of education."

"And then there's the inspiring story of Govindan Mestri," Professor continued, a smile playing on his lips. "Govindan, a skilled craftsman from Kollam, came to Sivagiri to repair a leaking building. Recognizing his dedication and expertise, the Guru blessed his work. Govindan's reputation as a reliable and skilled craftsman grew, and he soon became a successful contractor."

"The Guru, seeing Govindan's potential, advised him to start a tile manufacturing business," the Professor continued. "He even gave him a silver coin as a token of his support. Govindan established Lakshmi Vilasam Tiles, which flourished under his leadership, creating employment opportunities and contributing to the economic development of the region."

"These stories," Professor emphasized, "are not just about individual success; they're about the ripple effect of the Guru's influence on the economic landscape. He inspired and empowered individuals to become agents of change, creating opportunities not just for themselves but also for their communities."

"The Guru also encouraged established leaders to embrace entrepreneurship," Professor added. "Dr. Palpu, a key figure in the SNDP Yogam, established the Malabar Economic Union to promote the coir and copra industry, recognizing the potential of these traditional industries for economic growth. Mahakavi Kumaranasan, near Aluva another prominent leader, started Union Tile Works, demonstrating his commitment to the Guru's vision of economic self-reliance."

"These initiatives," Professor explained, "not only created economic opportunities but also served as models for others to emulate. They demonstrated that entrepreneurship was not just about profit but also about social responsibility and community development."

His message of empowerment and entrepreneurship resonated with people from all walks of life, transcending geographical boundaries." Inspired by the Guru's call for promoting economic activities, many of his believers in the modern age have established sustainable enterprise globally like the European countries, the USA, Canada, Singapore, Malaysia, the Middle East counties, and the African countries, apart from the major Cities and Towns in India.

"The Guru's legacy," Professor concluded, his voice filled with admiration, "is not just about spiritual enlightenment; it's about a holistic vision of progress that encompasses economic empowerment, social transformation, and the creation of a just and equitable society. The entrepreneurs created by the Guru were not just successful businessmen; they were pioneers, innovators, and agents of change, carrying forward his vision of a prosperous and enlightened world."

"And it's important to understand," Professor continued, his gaze sweeping across Mythili and Pavan, "that The Guru's economic philosophy wasn't about mere accumulation of wealth. It was about creating a sustainable and equitable economic ecosystem."

He elaborated on the concept of sustainable economics. "The Guru implicitly understood the interconnectedness of economic activity and social well-being. He advocated for industries that were not only profitable but also beneficial to the community and the environment.

He encouraged the use of local resources, the development of sustainable practices, and the fair distribution of wealth."

The Professor then focused on the importance of access to financial resources. "The Guru recognized that access to capital was crucial for aspiring entrepreneurs, particularly those from marginalized communities. That's why he supported the establishment of institutions like the Cochin National Bank. He understood that providing financial support, coupled with guidance and mentorship, could unlock the entrepreneurial potential of individuals who were traditionally excluded from economic opportunities."

The Professor then brought up the topic of skill development and training. "The Guru magnified the importance of skill development and training as essential components of entrepreneurship. He recognized that entrepreneurs needed not only capital but also the knowledge and skills to manage their businesses effectively. He encouraged the establishment of vocational training centers and educational institutions that could equip individuals with the skills they needed to succeed."

The Professor provided a practical example. "Consider the story of Govindan Mestri. He wasn't just a skilled craftsman; he was also a resourceful entrepreneur. But the Guru recognized that he needed more than just his skills to succeed. He needed guidance and support to build a sustainable business. By encouraging him to start a tile manufacturing company and providing him with a silver coin as a token of support, the Guru helped Govindan's transition from a skilled craftsman to a successful entrepreneur."

"And it wasn't just about starting new businesses," Professor continued. "The Guru also encouraged the modernization and expansion of existing industries. He understood that traditional industries like coir and handloom had the potential to generate significant economic opportunities if they were modernized and managed efficiently."

The Professor gave an example of the coir industry. "Dr. Palpu's initiative to establish the Malabar Economic Union was a testament to the Guru's vision for the modernization of traditional industries. By organizing coir producers and providing them with access to markets and technology, Dr. Palpu helped to revitalize the coir industry and to create new economic opportunities for thousands of people."

"Furthermore, the Guru emphasized the importance of ethical business practices," Professor stated. "He believed that businesses should be conducted with integrity and fairness, and that profits should be shared equitably with workers and the community. He condemned exploitation and corruption, and he advocated for a business culture that was based on trust and mutual respect."

"The Guru also understood the importance of diversification," Professor continued. "He encouraged entrepreneurs to explore new markets, develop new products, and diversify their businesses to mitigate risk and create new opportunities. He recognized that adaptability and innovation were essential for long-term success."

"In essence," Professor summarized, "The Guru's economic philosophy was a holistic approach that encompassed not just the creation of wealth but also the promotion of social well-being, environmental sustainability, and ethical business practices. He understood that true economic progress required a balanced and integrated approach that addressed the needs of individuals, communities, and the environment."

"The entrepreneurs molded by the Guru were not just business leaders," Professor punctuated. "They were social reformers, community builders, and agents of change. They were guided by a vision that extended beyond personal gain, a vision that sought to create a more just and equitable society. And their stories continue to inspire us today, reminding us that entrepreneurship can be a powerful force for solace in the world."

He paused, allowing his words to resonate, and then added, "The Guru's legacy is a reminder that economic empowerment is not just about creating jobs and generating wealth. It's about building a society where everyone has the opportunity to realize their full potential, to live a life of dignity and purpose. And that's a vision, that's as relevant today as it was a century ago."

As the sun began to dip below the horizon, casting long, golden shadows across the landscape, Professor led Mythili and Pavan towards a small, unassuming building nestled among the trees. "This," he said, his voice hushed with reverence, "is where the Guru spent many hours, meditating, reflecting, and formulating his vision for a transformed society."

Inside, the room was simple, almost austere. A single wooden desk, and a few chairs, and a small library of books comprised the furnishings. The air was still, imbued with a sense of peace and tranquility.

"The Guru's economic philosophy was not merely theoretical," Professor explained, gesturing towards the desk. "It was rooted in his deep understanding of the realities of life, his profound empathy for the suffering of others, and his unwavering belief in the potential of humanity."

He paused, allowing the silence to amplify his words, then continued, "He understood that economic empowerment was not just about providing material resources; it was about furthering a sense of self-worth, dignity, and agency."

He walked over to a small bookshelf and pulled out a worn volume. "The Guru's writings are filled with insights into the nature of work, wealth, and prosperity. He emphasized the importance of honest labor, the dignity of all professions, and the need to create a society where everyone had the opportunity to contribute their talents and skills."

He opened the book and read aloud a passage: "'Work is worship. To engage in honest labor is to serve God and humanity. True prosperity comes not from accumulating wealth but from using it wisely to benefit others.'

"The Guru understood that wealth was not an end in itself," the Professor explained. "It was a means to an end, a tool for creating a better world. He encouraged entrepreneurs to use their wealth to create jobs, support education, and promote social welfare."

He then addressed the crucial aspect of community development. "The Guru recognized that economic progress was inextricably linked to community development. He encouraged entrepreneurs to invest in their communities, to support local schools, hospitals, and infrastructure projects. He believed that strong, vibrant communities were essential for sustainable economic growth."

He shared a story: "When Govindan Mestri's tile manufacturing business flourished, he didn't just accumulate wealth for himself. He invested in his community, building schools and providing scholarships to deserving students. He understood that his success was intertwined with the well-being of his community."

The Professor then reinforced the importance of education and knowledge dissemination. "The Guru believed that education was the key to unlocking the potential of individuals and communities. He comforted entrepreneurs to support education initiatives, to provide training and mentorship to aspiring entrepreneurs, and to promote a culture of lifelong learning."

The Guru endorsed that knowledge was power, and he encouraged others to seek knowledge and use it to improve their lives and their communities."

The Professor then narrated about the role of technology and innovation. "The Guru, despite living in a time of limited technological advancement, recognized the importance of innovation and the adoption of new technologies. He encouraged entrepreneurs to embrace new ideas, to experiment with new methods, and to continuously improve their products and processes."

The Professor gave an example. "The success of Chandrika soap was not just due to its traditional Ayurvedic formulation. It was also due to Kesavan Vaidyan's innovative marketing strategies and his ability to adapt to changing market conditions."

The Professor then addressed the importance of collaboration and cooperation. "The Guru understood that economic progress was not a solitary endeavor. He encouraged entrepreneurs to collaborate, to form cooperatives and associations, and to work together to achieve common goals."

The Professor shared another story about the cooperative movement. "The Guru's support for the establishment of the Cochin National Bank was a testament to his belief in the power of cooperation. He understood that by pooling their resources and working together, individuals could achieve far more than they could on their own."

"The Guru's legacy is not just about individual success stories," Professor concluded, his voice filled with passion. "It's about a holistic vision of economic development that encompasses social responsibility, community development, and ethical business practices. It's about creating a society where everyone has the opportunity to thrive, to contribute, and to live a life of dignity and purpose."

The Professor looked at Mythili and Pavan, his eyes filled with hope. "The Guru's message is as relevant today as it was a century ago. In a world facing numerous economic and social challenges, his vision of a just and equitable society provides a guiding light, a roadmap for creating a better future for all."

As they stepped out of the building, the stars twinkled in the darkening sky, a silent testament to the enduring legacy of the Guru's vision, a vision that continues to inspire and empower generations.

Key Learnings from the study on entrepreneurship were summarized by Professor Shiva as:

- ***Emphasis on Industry:*** *The Guru actively promoted industry as a means for economic upliftment, encouraging individuals to establish businesses and contribute to societal prosperity.*
- ***Guidance and Empowerment:*** *The Guru provided direct guidance and blessings to individuals, enabling them to overcome obstacles and achieve entrepreneurial success, as seen in the stories of C.R. Kesavan Vaidyan (Chandrika Soap), M.P. Moothedath (railway contractor), and Govindan Mestri (Lakshmi Vilasam Tiles).*
- ***Diversification of Industries:*** *The Guru's influence led to the establishment of diverse industries, including Ayurvedic products (Chandrika, Medimix), construction (tiles, contracting), and financial institutions (Cochin National Bank), demonstrating his broad economic vision.*
- ***Ethical Entrepreneurship and Social Responsibility:*** *The entrepreneurs inspired by the Guru demonstrated a commitment to social responsibility, reinvesting their wealth in education, community development, and philanthropy.*
- ***Long-Term Economic Impact:*** *The Guru's teachings and actions spurred a wave of entrepreneurial activity, leading to the growth of numerous successful businesses and contributing significantly to the economic development of the region, with effects that reached beyond the region.*

22

Epilogue: The Sivagiri Pilgrimage – A Perpetual Cycle of Learning

The sun, a molten orb dipping towards the horizon, cast long shadows across the Sivagiri Hill, painting the landscape in hues of orange and gold. The air, alive with the rhythmic chants of pilgrims and the gentle rustling of leaves, carried a sense of both serenity and purpose. Professor, Mythili, and Pavan stood on the hilltop, their hearts filled with a profound sense of connection to the legacy of the Guru.

The Sivagiri Pilgrimage encapsulates Sree Narayana Guru's economic vision, uniting education, organization, and industry to foster a just society. The current work has explored how his principles — articulated a century ago — offer solutions to modern challenges, from poverty alleviation to sustainable development. It's a perpetual cycle of learning, reflection, and action, a journey towards both spiritual enlightenment and material progress."

The Professor gestured towards the pilgrims, their faces etched with devotion and determination. "Every year, thousands gather here, drawn by the teachings of the Guru, seeking inspiration and guidance. They come from all walks of life, representing the diversity of India, united by a common desire for a better future."

Mythili, her eyes reflecting the vibrant scene, asked, "Professor, how does the Sivagiri Pilgrimage embody the Guru's economic vision?"

"The Guru understood that true progress required a holistic approach," Professor explained. "He recognized the interconnectedness of spiritual, social, and economic well-being. The Sivagiri Pilgrimage, with its emphasis on education, organization, and industry, reflects this integrated vision."

The Professor then elaborated on the eight topics that the Guru had proposed for the pilgrimage conferences: education, cleanliness, devotion to God, organization, agriculture, trade, handicrafts, and technical training. "These topics," Professor said, "represent the key pillars of the Guru's vision for a transformed society. They encompass both the spiritual and the material aspects of human existence, recognizing that true prosperity can only be achieved through a balanced and harmonious development of both."

Pavan, his gaze fixed on the pilgrims, asked, "Professor, how does the pilgrimage contribute to the ongoing Sivagiri model, where people learn new things every year?

"The pilgrimage is a dynamic platform for knowledge sharing and learning," Professor replied. "Every year, experts in various fields are invited to deliver lectures and conduct workshops on the eight topics. This ensures that the pilgrimage remains relevant to the changing times and that the knowledge imparted is up-to-date and practical."

The Professor then highlighted the importance of continuous learning. "The Guru believed that education was not just a one-time event but a lifelong process. He emphasized the importance of continuous learning, adaptation, and innovation. The Sivagiri Pilgrimage, with its annual cycle of knowledge sharing, embodies this principle."

The Professor then shared a personal anecdote. "I remember attending a pilgrimage conference a few years ago," he said, "where an expert in sustainable agriculture spoke about the latest techniques in organic farming. The farmers in the audience were fascinated, and many of them adopted these techniques, leading to increased yields and improved livelihoods. This is just one example of how the pilgrimage contributes to the ongoing Sivagiri model."

The Professor then emphasized the importance of collective action. "The Guru believed that organization was crucial for achieving social and economic progress. He encouraged people to form cooperatives, associations, and unions to collectively address their challenges and work towards common goals.[2] The Sivagiri Pilgrimage, with its emphasis on organization, reinforces this principle."[3]

The Professor then highlighted the role of the pilgrimage in promoting entrepreneurship. "The Guru recognized the importance of entrepreneurship in driving economic growth. He stimulated individuals to start their businesses, to innovate, and to create opportunities for themselves and their communities. The Sivagiri Pilgrimage, with its focus on industry, trade, and handicrafts, provides a platform for aspiring entrepreneurs to learn, network, and showcase their products and services."

The Professor then shared another episode. "Last year, I met Priya, a young entrepreneur at the pilgrimage, who launched 'Eco-Glow,' a line of organic soaps inspired by the Guru's sustainability teachings. After attending a workshop on digital marketing, she scaled her business online, creating jobs for ten women in her village."

The Professor then stressed the importance of social responsibility. "The Guru believed that economic progress should not come at the expense of social justice and environmental sustainability. He advocated for ethical business practices, fair wages, and the protection of natural resources. The Sivagiri Pilgrimage, with its focus on cleanliness, devotion to God, and community development, reinforces these principles."

He then highlighted the role of the pilgrimage in promoting environmental awareness. "The Guru was a pioneer in promoting nature conservation. He recognized the interconnectedness of human well-being and environmental health. The Sivagiri Pilgrimage, with its emphasis on cleanliness and sustainable practices, continues to raise awareness about environmental issues and promote responsible stewardship of our planet."

The Professor Siva then concluded, his voice filled with conviction, "The Sivagiri Pilgrimage is a living testament to the Guru's economic vision of a transformed society. It's a perpetual cycle of learning, reflection, and action, a journey towards both spiritual enlightenment and material progress. It's a beacon of hope, a reminder that true prosperity can only be achieved through a balanced and harmonious development of all aspects of human existence."

As the sun dipped below the horizon, casting a final golden glow across the Sivagiri Hill, Mythili and Pavan felt a profound sense of gratitude for the legacy of the Guru. They comprehended that the Sivagiri Pilgrimage was not just an annual event but a continuous process of learning, growth, and transformation, a journey that would continue to inspire and guide them on their path towards a better future.

The Sivagiri Pilgrimage, with its emphasis on education, organization, and industry, serves as a perpetual reminder of the Guru's economic vision. It's a dynamic platform for knowledge sharing, a catalyst for entrepreneurship, and a beacon of social responsibility. It's a testament to the enduring power of the Guru's teachings, a legacy that continues to shape the economic landscape of Kerala and beyond.

❖ ❖ ❖

APPENDIX 1

KOLATHIRESASTHAVAM

Composed in 1893 for devotees at Kolathukara, *Kolathireswasthavam* reflects the Guru's holistic vision. Its plea to alleviate poverty (Verse 7) underscores his economic concern for the marginalized, aligning with his advocacy for self-reliance and community support. Tradition holds that the universal, all-pervading Absolute becomes manifested locally for the benefit of devotees. Many old poems in this style exist.

1.

Favourable to those who seek refuge from death,
forehead-eyed, fully against those unrighteous,
O, supreme Lord, reigning in the temple of Kolathukara.
protect me well now.

2.

Creating the whole world in a wink,
Who, by mere look rules over all, forever;
He who plays these games, the supreme Lord,
reigning in the temple of Kolathukara, may He protect me.

3.

Shelter for all, filling everywhere, who wears this form
for His devotees to meditate on,
remove my inertia, grant ultimate awareness,
O, supreme Lord, reigning in the temple of Kolathukara.

4.

This eye and other senses, if any of them,
thoughtlessly gets onto an untrue path,
right there, give rise to true thoughts in me,
O, supreme Lord, reigning in the temple of Kolathukara.

5.

Hands and legs, or my other limbs, may they never act untrue,
may I not attempt, by un-wisdom,
what should not be done; make me thus,
O, supreme Lord, reigning in the temple of Kolathukara.

6.

Remove all ailments and sorrows, please do,
O granter of desires, burner of desires, O milk-ocean of kindness,
grant me well-being, O Sambhu,
supreme Lord, reigning in the temple of Kolathukara.

7.

Poverty's great misery, may it never afflict me,
may deluded ego stay far away,
may good fortune come to me to stay close to kindly people,
O, supreme Lord, reigning in the temple of Kolathukara.

8.

Heal the faults done inconsiderately,
remove my burning sorrows, protect me, and moreover,
may I, daily, come to remember Your word, that removes all evil,
O, supreme Lord, reigning in the temple of Kolathukara.

9.

For the ordained ordainer Brahma, and even for the immeasurable Vishnu,
O, timeless One, who can describe your magnificence
I just spoke some of my wishes,
O, supreme Lord, reigning in the temple of Kolathukara.

10

Like a baby in pain with no words to tell it,
even thus is my meaningless prattle here;
You are the basis, ever together with mother, do come,
O, supreme Lord, reigning in the temple of Kolathukara.

[This is a translated version from Malayalam to English by Vinaya Chaitanya]

APPENDIX 2

DAIVA DASAKAM

(Universal Prayer]

Written in Malayalam, this is a simple prayer that the Guru composed for the use of children at the Sanskrit school he had founded. Though simple at first reading, it is a treasury of wisdom and is a condensed version of the teachings of the ten major Upanishads. Written in 1914, this prayer summarizes the teachings of the Upanishads in ten verses.

1

0, God, from there beyond,
keep watch on us here
never letting go Your hand;
You are the captain and
Your word,* a mighty steamboat
for this sea of change.

[*Padam, which has been rendered as 'word' here, can also mean 'feet' as well as 'state of being']

2.

When all things - touched
and counted, one by one - end,
then the seeing eye stops, still.
In like manner, may the inside
become still and settle in You.

3.

Giving us food, clothes, and such,
without lapse, You preserve us,
making us generously blessed.
You alone are our true Master.

4.

Inwardly seen,
we are like the ocean, and
maya is like the wave.
the wind is your glory and
the depths, you Yourself

5.

You verily are creation and creator,
and the magical web of creatures, too.
are You not, O God, the very stuff
of which all creation is made?

6

You alone are *Maya*, the conjurer of *Maya*,
and the enjoyer of *Maya*. Are you not, also
the great One, who, removing *Maya*,
will grant the supreme union?

7.

You are truth, knowledge, and happiness,
You alone are the present,
past and future, too, are none other;
the spoken word, when
remembered, is also You.

8.

Glorious is your word which fills
both inside and outside, to the brim.
That alone we praise,
O gracious God, ever victorious.

9.

Yours is the victory,
O great God, ever intent on saving those in misery;
You alone triumph, all-knowing joy,
ocean of mercy, praise be to You!

10

In the ocean of Your glory of
ever-increasing depth. May we all
together. Get immersed and remain
there forever. In Happiness.

***[This is a translated version from Malayalam to English by Vinaya Chaitanya*]**

APPENDIX 3

DHARMA

This short verse in Sanskrit, was written invoking blessings for a new journal of the same name, started by some of his disciples. Dharma - from the root 'dhri', to support, to bear, from which the word for earth is also derived -is the law of what is naturally right. Firmly established virtue, true morality, religion and duty are all implied in this word; it is also to be understood in the context of svadharma, or one's own dharma.

Dharma alone is the supreme divinity,
dharma indeed is the greatest wealth,
may dharma triumph everywhere
for the well-being of humanity

[This is a translated version from Sanskrit to English by Vinaya Chaitanya]

Bibliography

Books in English

Alexander, P. C. (1949). *Buddhism in Kerala.* Annamalai University, Annamalai Nagar

Gopinathan, G. (2024). *Sri Narayana Guru: Pioneer of Spiritual Revolution.* Mathrubhumi, Kozhikode

Kotler, P., & Lee, N. (2009). *Corporate Social Responsibility.* Scientific Research Publishing, Glendale, USA

Muni Narayana Prasad. (2008). *The Philosophy of Narayana Guru.* D.K. Print World Ltd., New Delhi

Nancy Yeilding. (2017). *Narayana Guru: life of Liberating Love* , D.K. Printworld Pvt. Ltd., New Delhi

Nataraja Guru, (2007). *The Word of Guru.* Pai & Co., Ernakulam, India

Ravindran T. K. (1972). *Asan and Social Revolution in Kerala.* Kerala Historical Society, Thiruvananthapuram

Sadasivan S. N. (2000). *A Social History of India.* APH Publishers Corporation, New Delhi

Sarngadharan, M. (Ed) (1999). *Platinum Jubilee Celebration of All Religion Conference -Aluva.* Sree Narayana Dharma Sangham Trust, Sivagiri

Sasidharan, G.K. (2020). *Not Many But One Vol. 1: Sree Narayana G: Sree Narayana Guru's Philosophy of Universal Oneness*. Penguin Viking

Thurston Edger. (1975). *Caste and tribes of Southern India.* Cosmo Publications, Delhi

Yunus, M. (2007) Creating a World without Poverty: Social Business and the Future of Capitalism. Public Affairs, New York

Books in Malayalam

Balakrishnan, P. K. (1954). *Narayana guru - Collected Works* (Malayalam). National Book Stall, Kottayam

Balakrishnan, P. K. (1969). *Narayana guru - Collected Works* (Malayalam). NBS, Kottayam

Balarama Panikkar, K. (2008). *Through the Writings of Sreenarayanaguru*(Malayalam). Shivagiri Mutt Publications, Sivagiri

Bhaskaran, T. (1965). *Sreenarayanaguru, Complete Works of Sree Narayana Guru, (Explanation of Vidyothini, Bhaskaran T.* Dr.) (Malayalam). Mathrubhumi, Kozhikode

Gopalakrishnan, P. K. (1974). *Cultural History of Kerala* (Malayalam). Kerala Bhasha Institute, Thiruvananthapuram

Gopalakrishnan, P. K. (1991). *Cultural History of Kerala*. (Malayalam). Kerala Bhasha Institute, Thiruvananthapuram

Kerala Kaumudi. (2007). *Sree Narayana Guru Directory* (Malayalam), Kerala Kaumudi Publications, Thiruvananthapuram, India

Kumaran, Moorkkothu. (1998). *Sree Narayana Guru's Biography* (Malayalam). Sree Narayana Dharma Samgam Trust, Sivagiri, Vakala

Latha, Gopalakrishnan, (Ed). (2024). *Sree Narayana Bhakthosa: M.P. Moothedath*. (Malayalam). Ivory Books, Thrissur

Damodaran, K. (2003). *Life History of Sri Narayana Guru* (Malayalam). Kaumudi Publications, Thiruvananthapuram

Nair, Balakrishnan, G. (2007). *Sri Narayana Guru Deva's Works- Complete Commentary* (Malayalam). Kerala Bhasha Institute, Thiruvananthapuram

Rao, S. N. Muthalper. (2015). *Revolution: In Marx and Sreenarayan Guru.* (Malayalam). Rishikulam Publications Kizhillam

Sanu M.K., (1976). *Narayanaguruswami*(Malayalam).Vivekodayam, Irinjalakuda

Sarngadharan M. (2023). *Vaikom Satyagraha and the Kerala Renaissance - A few Historical Realitie,* (Malayalam). Melinda Books, Thiruvananthapuram

Sarngadharan M. (2024). *Sree Narayana Guru's Economic Vision* (Malayalam). Maithri Books, Thiruvananthapuram

Sarngadharan M. (2025). *Current Relevance of Sivagrimage Topics.* (Malayalam). Maithri Books, Thiruvananthapuram

Sarngadharan M. (Ed). (1998). *Tirthaswana.* (Malayalam). Sree Narayana Dharma Sangham Trust, Shivagiri

Sarngadharan M. (Ed). (1999) *Vaikom Satyagraha and Gandhi.* (Malayalam). Sree Narayana Dharma Sangham Trust, Shivagiri

Sarngadharan M. (Ed). (1999). *TirthadanaChinthakal.* (Malayalam). Sree Narayana Dharma Sangham Trust, Shivagiri

Sarngadharan M. (Ed). (2023) *Sree Narayana Guru and the Interfaith Conference.* (Malayalam). Maithri Books, Thiruvananthapuram

Sugathan, K. (2007). *History of Guru* (Malayalam). Sreenarayana Club, Kozhikode

Vinayakumar, L. (2021). *Sri Narayana Guru and the Modern Society of Kerala* (Malayalam). Kalapurna Publications, Varkala